SYMBOL

The wheat of the world
Is a woman of grace;
She is supple and strong
With the sun on her face.
Like a goddess she beckons
With confident air;
Men follow and worship
The gold in her hair.

– Ruth Bransford Wilson

A *Romance*

W ITH

B AKING

A MILLENNIUM
DEDICATION
TO THE AMERICAN
FLOUR MILLING
INDUSTRY

BY KAROL REDFERN HAMPER

WITH THE SPECIAL ASSISTANCE AND ARTISTIC COLLABORATION OF SHELLEY ODEGARD

BOOK LAYOUT AND DESIGN BY COOPER EDENS AND SACHEVERELL DARLING

COVER DESIGN BY DOUG FAST AND JOE TSCHIDA

FOOD PHOTOGRAPHY BY MARK GORDON AND DAVE EMERY

OLD MILL PHOTOGRAPHY BY ROBERT CUSHMAN HAYES

IN LOVING MEMORY OF
"OMA"
RUTH LESH HAMPER
1918-1998
For the love you have shown my children, Kris and Jessica.

ISBN 0-9674772-0-4

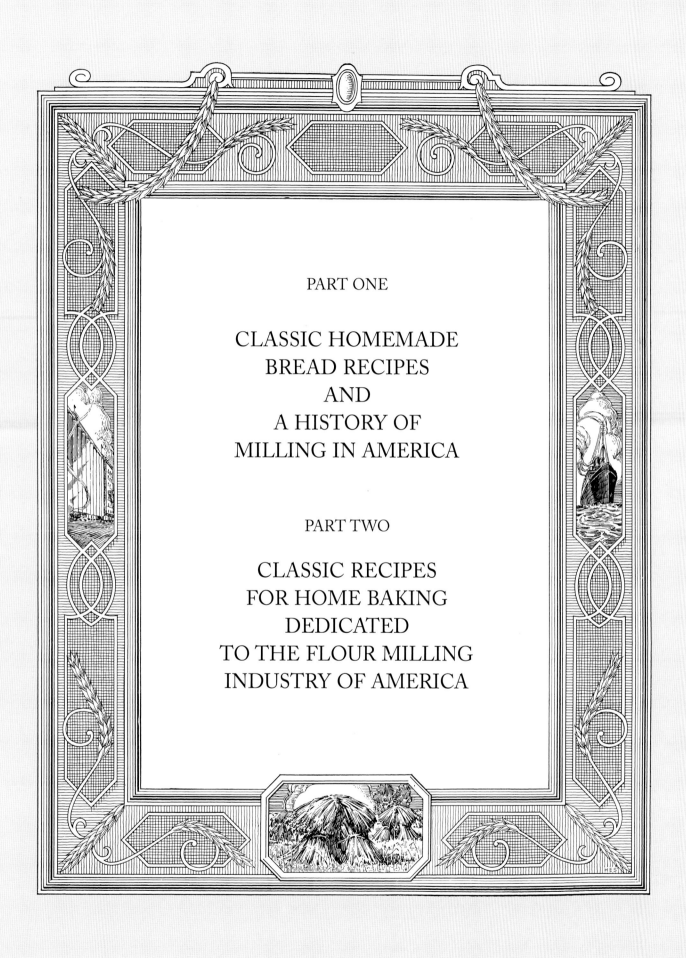

PART ONE

CLASSIC HOMEMADE
BREAD RECIPES
AND
A HISTORY OF
MILLING IN AMERICA

PART TWO

CLASSIC RECIPES
FOR HOME BAKING
DEDICATED
TO THE FLOUR MILLING
INDUSTRY OF AMERICA

FIRST CHOICE

What lovely things are golden–
The sun that gives us life,
Buttercups and jonquils,
The ring worn by a wife,
Canary birds and corn ears,
Cream thick enough to eat,
But loveliest of golden things
Are fields of shining wheat!

– Gates Hebbard

INTRODUCTION

Romance is more than falling in love, more than the tenderness shared by lovers…Romance is the journey we take with our heart, spurred by the passion that fills us with indescribable joy as we explore our interests in people, places, and the things we love. That passion gives us the feeling that some wonderful treasure awaits us and just begs to be discovered and enjoyed.

Little did I know, ten years ago when I embarked upon this venture, that my research would unveil bound volume sets of the American Miller, a monthly newspaper, and the Northwestern Miller, published weekly, dating from their inception in 1873. Numerous flour milling journals were in existence in the late 1800's, but by the middle of the 1900's only these two remained.

Millers and bakers throughout America submitted stories and informative articles to these predominant publications. Their wives sent in their favorite poems, passionately depicting their romance with baking and affectionate recollections of milling's past. The American Miller endured 95 years and The Northwestern Miller's reign lasted 100 years. These fascinating and highly significant publications formed the foundation of my work.

Flour is the inherent soul in baked goods. This baking book features over 100 commemorative recipes, from breads to pastries, cheesecakes to pies. It begins with The Renaissance of Wheat, exploring the ancient and honorable craft of flour milling, from the earliest times to the present, while featuring the history, stories, poetry and lore, from others who share in the majesty and sentiment of wheat and bread and in the baking romance.

Few are the bakers that have not wondered about the mysteries of this food: a descendant of ancient Asian grasses-the cultivation of wheat, ground and purified into flour. The baker is conscious, at one time or another, of the great satisfaction he takes in his labor, which transcends all drudgery and weariness. To some, there is a spiritual and esoteric meaning in the act of mixing a batch of dough, as if they were performing a sacred rite.

This book is a dedication to the grower of the wheat, the miller, and the baker; a reflection and a long overdue recognition of the service and dedication of those people who bring us our daily bread. Come join me in a peek from the present into the romantic past. Come smell the bread baking.

Karol Redfern Hamper

The Miller Wooing

PART ONE

CLASSIC HOMEMADE BREAD RECIPIES
AND A HISTORY OF MILLING IN AMERICA

THE RENAISSANCE OF WHEAT

BEAUTY'S SELF

I saw today, if not her face –
Too blinding, that–at least the grace
Of slim form swathed in gold gauze lace.

Beauty's self–How else explain
An expanse of rippling grain
Shimmer-gossamered after rain?

– Ethel Romig Fuller

The mystery of wheat is the subject of legend in many cultures. Among the Egyptians and Greeks, wheat was a gift of the gods. For the Chinese, it was a grant from heaven, celebrated by an annual sowing, in which the Emperor himself participated. Almost all of the early religious beliefs regarded wheat as a symbol of life and they glorified the harvest and venerated bread as the gift of the gods.

Our present knowledge of botany lends us to believe that the wheat now in cultivation was derived from one or more species of wild Asian grasses. The first harvest probably took place between 15,000 and 10,000 B.C. As man has depended upon wheat for his sustenance, wheat has depended upon man for its propagation. Never has wheat been found where it is not bound up with human work. Its planting, cultivation and harvest are inseparably a part of human history.

The discovery of cereal grains transformed primitive man from a hunter and wanderer to a homesteader. At first, the branch of a tree was dragged back and forth over the field to level the ground, and then the grain was scattered from a bag slung around the farmer's shoulder. At harvest time, this ancient farmer pulled the plants up by hand and broke off the heads. Soon a sickle of iron or bronze was developed to cut the wheat close to the ground so that it could be bound into sheaves. Threshing was performed by hand with sticks or by driving cattle over the grain to loosen the heads while the wind carried off the chaff.

A gain in years and experience developed larger acreage and better yields. This universal grain, above all others, most comfortably adjusts itself to the needs and the dietary customs of the populations of the varied countries. ("Bread" is, in fact, a generic name for anything made from flour, moistened with water or milk, either with or without leaven, baked or boiled.) Caravans of camels transported surplus wheat along the banks of the Nile or the Euphrates to exchange for the fruits and fabrics of distant tribes. With this traffic of wheat came new knowledge and geography. Trade routes were established and invention and exploration followed.

The United States is by far one of the largest producers and exporters of wheat today. With the golden grain fields waving in the breezes, or the shocks of the harvested grain standing like sentinels to ward off famine, or a stream of golden grain flowing from the thresher's spout, comes a new zest and spirit of prosperity. The world's counting houses and kitchens look expectantly toward the American harvest for the signal that all is well for another year. The pulse of "the street" and the spirit of the home are quickened and renewed when the message comes that the harvest will be sufficient unto the need.

Summer, The Gleaners

BREAD TIPS & TERMINOLOGY

FLOUR PROTEIN

The "all-purpose flour" called for in this book contains protein within the 9.5 to 11 percent range. This is the standard that is recognized by the millers and is the most available flour for home baking.

OPTIMUM CONDITIONS FOR YEAST

Yeast is a living organism, a microscopic plant. When the right conditions are offered to the yeast, the yeast plants begin to grow and multiply very fast. This growth process produces a leavening gas, or carbon dioxide, which gets trapped in the gluten, the tiny network of fibers that are formed when the dough is mixed or kneaded. This network helps hold in the gasses that are released from the yeast as it develops, and causes the dough to rise. This increase of volume improves the grain and texture in our baked goods.

To properly activate yeast, water, nutrients and the correct temperature are the three ingredients needed. The two forms yeast comes in are compressed cake and dry. Crumble the cake, or sprinkle the dry yeast into warm water, between 90 to 115 degrees. The optimum temperature for yeast is 110 degrees. If the temperature is much cooler, the yeast remains dormant. If the temperature is hotter, the yeast may die. If you add any ingredients to the yeast dough that have been heated, such as milk, potatoes or grains, be sure that they have cooled to barely warm.

Adding a small amount of sugar or honey to the yeast water helps feed the yeast and bring it to life. It should, within the next 20 minutes, start to foam in the cup or bowl. If it does not come to life, don't use it in your baking. This could mean the temperature of the water was too hot or the yeast was too old.

EQUIVALENT

When the recipes in this chapter call for one tablespoon of yeast, one envelope of dry yeast or one cake of compressed yeast is the equivalent.

SPONGE METHOD

Most of the breads in this chapter incorporate the "sponge method," a few basic fundamental principles that can be applied to any yeast bread recipe to give you optimum results. A sponge is made by placing the water, yeast, soaked grains, any specialty flours or other listed ingredients in the particular recipe into a large bowl, then adding only enough of the remaining flour to make a thick mud. This mud is stirred to incorporate air and to help develop the gluten, which is essential in good bread.

A rest period follows which does wonders for the dough. It allows the dough time to knead itself, which helps further develop the gluten. Less flour will then need to be incorporated during the final kneading process, which will give you a lighter bread. This rest period also gives the flour a chance to soak up some of the water, so it contains moisture and doesn't pull more moisture from the final finished product.

BREAD TIPS & TERMINOLOGY

YEAST RETARDERS

Oil and salt are known to be yeast retarders, which means they inhibit, or slow down the growth progress of the yeast. This is why they should be added after the yeast is activated and the sponge has had the opportunity to develop.

KNEADING

The amount of flour needed during the final kneading process is always a variable. The more you knead the dough, the more the gluten is developed. The more the loaf is bound together, by the gluten; less flour need be incorporated. This makes for a lighter, smoother product. Adding too much flour can cause the bread to be heavy and dry, so add only enough flour to make it a workable dough.

PUNCHING DOWN

After the dough has doubled in volume in the bowl, punch the dough down to bring beneficial oxygen to the yeast and work out any air bubbles. This is done by pushing your fist into the middle of the dough and working the dough into a ball by bringing the outer edges of the dough into the center and kneading briefly.

PREHEATING THE OVEN

Be sure to preheat your oven in plenty of time so that it will be the correct temperature before your bread goes in. If you start preheating it too late, the bread may get "over proofed" and have holes in the texture. Under desirable conditions, the yeast in the dough converts the natural sugar in the flour into food, then releases a gas which makes the bread rise. If the dough is allowed to rise too long before it is put into the oven, this food source is diminished. The yeast then converts the flour into sugar and slowly consumes it, leaving the once rounded top looking collapsed, or, depending on when it went into the oven, there could be large air bubbles in the top that you will notice when the bread is sliced.

If the oven temperature is not hot enough, the yeast becomes overly active and speeds the converting process. The correct oven temperature kills the yeast and the dough keeps its good grain and texture.

EGG WASH

Egg white, mixed with a little water and brushed on the loaves before baking gives them a shiny crust and also helps any oats, seeds or nuts to adhere. Egg yolk mixed with water gives the loaves a golden color. Be sure to mix well and carefully brush the loaves evenly so they will brown uniformly. For a soft crust, rub the tops with butter when the loaves are removed from the oven.

OVEN SPRING AND CHOOSING THE CORRECT PAN

"Oven spring" is the term used to describe what happens to the yeast during the beginning stages of the baking process when it is activated by heat. As the temperature rises in the dough, the yeast speeds up the process of converting the sugar in the flour into food, consuming it and giving off a carbon dioxide gas. The dough expands rapidly for a short while, until the heat becomes too hot and the yeast is destroyed.

BREAD TIPS & TERMINOLOGY

The dough needs enough room in the pan to almost double before going into the oven, and along with the estimated amount of "oven spring," take on a well-proportioned domed look. Be sure to use shortening to grease your pans. Oil makes them stick, and butter, because of its low burning point, makes them burn.

CHECKING FOR DONENESS

When baking bread at home you really don't need a clock. A good test for doneness is to wait for the bread to start letting off its heavenly aroma, which is its own built in reminder. Check the bread, then if it looks done and the loaves sound hollow when tapped, carefully lift the loaves from the pans and check the sides. They too should be a golden color. If they are not, the loaves might collapse after they are removed from the pans. Carefully return the loaves to the pans and return them to the oven and check again every 5 to 10 minutes.

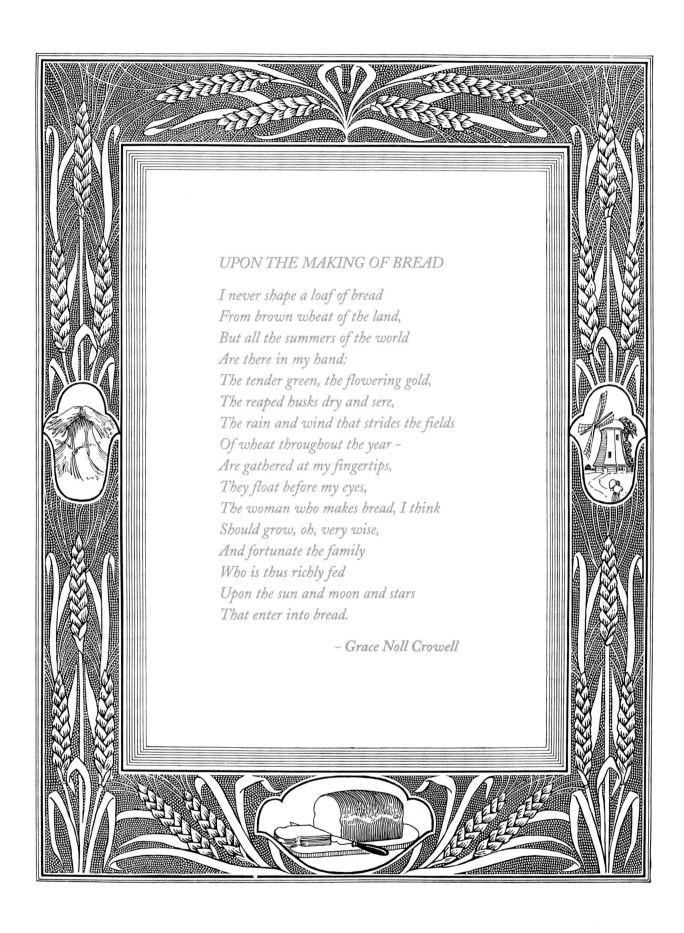

UPON THE MAKING OF BREAD

I never shape a loaf of bread
From brown wheat of the land,
But all the summers of the world
Are there in my hand:
The tender green, the flowering gold,
The reaped husks dry and sere,
The rain and wind that strides the fields
Of wheat throughout the year –
Are gathered at my fingertips,
They float before my eyes,
The woman who makes bread, I think
Should grow, oh, very wise,
And fortunate the family
Who is thus richly fed
Upon the sun and moon and stars
That enter into bread.

– Grace Noll Crowell

EARLY MILLING

Among all the industries of the world, flour milling may justly claim to have the longest continuous existence. The origin of wheat growing and flour milling goes back many centuries, beyond the reach of written or even pictured records. The first tales of milling appear in the written records of antiquity as already ancient institutions, vested in many cases with a profound religious significance.

Wheat was unquestionably used for human food in the earliest days of primitive mankind, and wherever grain was so used, there too developed the germ of flour milling. The first mill was most likely a depression in a rock where grain could be crushed with a stone by Neolithic man, who roasted his grains to make them more edible.

Through the passage of time, the "pounding stone" became more pointed, and the "bedstone" became more cup-shaped. These forms were accentuated, creating the "pestle and mortar". The grain was put into a hollow surface and rubbed by a round rolling-pin-like stone with a twisting motion, thus rubbing and bruising the grain as well as crushing it. Little by little, the rubbing part of the process increased in relative importance, until the entire work of reducing the grain to meal was accomplished by this method.

The "saddlestone," the earliest form of the real grinding mill, belongs to the dawn of recorded history. Chaldea was a cradle of civilization at the heart of an area which included Babylon, Nineveh, Assyria, Egypt and Persia. They created the saddlestone to grind corn, and it remains one of the world's pre-eminent milling tools. It was the first contrivance by which grinding, as distinguished from pounding, was made possible. It has survived through history and is in use to this day. Not even the common "quern," which came later, possesses that distinction.

The quern is a tool upon which the handle is fixed to the pestle, so that it could be turned round on the mortar. It is distinguished from the more primitive grain stones primarily by its circular motion, the upper stone revolving upon or with a pin upon the lower. This meant that the two stones remained in continuous contact, resulting in greater capacity and probably better ground meal. From walking round and round his mill, man harnessed an ass to the handle of the rotary mill, and the first step in power milling had been taken. This development resulted from a desire to economize by lightening the intensive human labor required in milling. The immense mechanical superiority of the revolving mill gradually established it as the pre-eminent milling device and made the production of grain in larger quantities possible.

AMERICA'S FIRST MILLERS

America's first millers were Indian women, grinding grains for their family while the men hunted. With her basic methods of grinding corn into meal, the Indian woman performed one of the most important functions of her tribe.

Some Native Americans used wooden pestles and hollowed trees to pound their corn. Early Indians also pounded their corn in basin-like depressions chipped in stationary rocks, using a pestle consisting of a stone with a rounded end. Stone mills were too heavy to be carried by the nomadic tribes, so the wandering Indians would barter with the gardening Indians for the ground corn meal.

The early settlers brought to the American colonies brought wheat, oats, rye, and barley. The colonists started growing wheat immediately. The beginning of a settlement consisted of a school, a church, and a mill. Quite commonly, the settlers created mills by burning or gouging out cavities from hardwood trees to make a mortar. They then used a wooden pestle to grind the corn or grains.

All early corn and grist mills were small and crude. They ground only three bushels per day, and the meal was not separated from the bran. Although grist was anything taken to the mill to be ground, the grist mill was first a corn mill. Later, when it became possible to balance the millstones to grind wheat, the mill was called a flouring mill. Such a mill produced whole wheat flour. Bolting, which separates the flour from the bran and middlings, was developed. The next great step forward in milling history was the application of a harnessed natural force, the use of "wind and water power" in milling.

WHOLESOME WHOLE WHEAT BREAD

YIELD : 2 LOAVES

3 CUPS WARM WATER
2 TABLESPOONS DRY YEAST
¼ CUP HONEY
3½ CUPS WHOLE WHEAT FLOUR
1 CUP POWDERED MILK
½ CUP BUTTER
1¼ TABLESPOONS SALT
4 CUPS UNBLEACHED, ALL-PURPOSE FLOUR
FLOUR FOR DUSTING THE BOARD
OIL FOR THE BOWL

THREE THINGS REMEMBERED

All things remembered have a life
Within themselves, and in the heart
Where sight and smell and sound can play
A strange and eager part.
For these return like melodies,
Insistent as a loved refrain,
I sense the smoke, the blossoms red
The gold-encompassed fields of grain,
And woodsmoke, roses after rain
And the smell of baking bread.

- Allen E. Woodall

TO PREPARE THE DOUGH

Pour the warm water into a large mixing bowl, sprinkle the yeast over it and stir in the honey. In a separate bowl, thoroughly mix together the 3½ cups of whole wheat flour and the powdered milk. This important step insures there won't be any lumps of powdered milk in the dough. Add the flour mixture to the dissolved yeast mixture stirring in a clockwise circular motion until smooth. Beat in the same direction 200 strokes. This helps the yeast to form the gluten which is essential in good bread. Cover with a clean tea towel and let this sponge rest 30 to 60 minutes, or until it starts to rise.

Melt the butter in a small saucepan and allow it to cool. When it has cooled to warm, pour it into the sponge, along with the salt, and beat again in the same circular direction until they are incorporated.

Beat in, one cup at a time, the 4 cups of all-purpose flour. On a lightly floured board, knead the dough 5 to 10 minutes until smooth and elastic, dusting the board with enough white flour from time to time to keep the dough from sticking. Place the dough in a clean, lightly oiled bowl, turning it once to oil the top. Cover the bowl and let the dough rise until it has doubled.

TO SHAPE AND BAKE

Lightly grease 2 large or 3 medium-size bread pans. Punch down the dough and knead briefly to remove any air bubbles. Divide the dough into 2 to 3 loaves, depending on the size of your pans. Shape the loaves and give them smooth, rounded tops. Place them, seam side down in the prepared pans. Cover and let rise until almost doubled.

While the dough is rising, preheat the oven to 375 degrees. Bake the loaves in the fully preheated oven for 40 to 50 minutes, or until they are a rich brown, the sides are lightly browned, and they sound hollow when tapped. The bread will have better texture if it is allowed to cool somewhat before slicing.

HOMEMADE WHITE BREAD

YIELD: 2 LOAVES

A SLICE OF BREAD

Mother, what makes bread so white?
Seed slept under snow, its winter-long night.
Why is the loaf so crusty and brown?
On fields, summer-through sun shone down.
Why is it so sweet? Because thirsty grain
Drank often from pitchers of dewdrops and rain.
Isn't bread interesting? Child, it should be;
In the slice you are eating is all history.

- Ethel Romig Fuller

1 MEDIUM POTATO
WATER TO COVER
1 TABLESPOON DRY YEAST
1 CUP MILK
2 TABLESPOONS SUGAR
2 EGGS
3 CUPS UNBLEACHED
   ALL-PURPOSE FLOUR
1 TEASPOON SALT
2 CUPS UNBLEACHED ALL-PURPOSE FLOUR
¾ CUP FLOUR FOR KNEADING (APPROXIMATELY)
VEGETABLE OIL FOR YOUR HANDS AND BOWL

TO PREPARE THE DOUGH

Wash and peel the potato and cut it into ½ inch cubes. In a small sauce pan, cover the potato cubes with water, cover and cook until very soft. Strain and reserve the cooking liquid, adding more if necessary, so that you have exactly ½ cup. When the potato liquid has cooled to warm, pour it into a large mixing bowl and sprinkle the yeast over it. Whip the potatoes with a small whisk until very smooth.

Scald the milk, then stir the sugar into it. When the milk mixture has cooled to warm, beat in the eggs. When the yeast mixture is foamy, pour the milk mixture into the yeast and beat with a wooden spoon in a continuous clockwise circular motion to blend. When you're sure the potatoes are creamy and have cooled to warm, measure out ½ cup and add it to the batter, beating again in a continuous clockwise circular motion. (You may want to rice the potatoes through a strainer to be positive there are no lumps).

Beat in, one cup at a time, the 3 cups of all-purpose flour until the batter is smooth and continue beating in the same clockwise circular motion for 200 strokes. Let this sponge rest, covered, for 30 minutes or until the batter starts to rise. After the sponge has started to rise, beat in the salt and the 2 cups of all-purpose flour until well incorporated. Pour this mixture out onto a well floured board. Wash and oil your hands lightly and start kneading the dough, adding small amounts of flour to the board to keep the dough from sticking. The potatoes in the dough make this dough a little stickier than other doughs, so try to keep your hands clean and lightly oiled. Knead for 5 to 10 minutes or until the dough is smooth and elastic.

Place the dough in a lightly oiled bowl, turning once to oil the top. Cover with a clean tea towel and let rise until doubled.

TO SHAPE AND BAKE

Lightly grease two medium-size bread pans. After the dough has doubled in volume, lightly oil your hands, punch the dough down and knead out any air bubbles. Divide the dough in half and shape the dough into two loaves. Place the loaves into the prepared pans, making sure they have smooth, rounded tops. Cover with a clean tea towel and let rise until almost doubled. Preheat the oven to 375 degrees. Bake the loaves in the fully preheated oven for 40 to 50 minutes, or until browned and the loaves sound hollow when tapped. Cool to warm before slicing.

FRESH BAKED BREAD

The savory scent of fresh-baked bread
Permeates a house
With fragrance lovlier than May
On crab apple boughs;

More titillant than tang in fall
Of smoke from leaf fires burning;
Than peaches in the August sun;
Than loam a plow is turning.

O more to be desired than red
Rose petals packed in cloves-
The perfume on a winter day
Of warm white wheaten loaves!

- Ethel Romig Fuller

EIGHT WHOLE GRAIN BREAD

YIELD: 2 LOAVES

2 CUPS WATER

½ CUP UNCOOKED 7-GRAIN CEREAL

2 TABLESPOONS BUTTER

¼ CUP HONEY

1 CUP WARM WATER

2 TABLESPOONS DRY YEAST

1 CUP WHOLE WHEAT FLOUR

1 CUP UNBLEACHED,
    ALL-PURPOSE FLOUR

1 TABLESPOON SALT

2 CUPS UNBLEACHED,
    ALL-PURPOSE FLOUR

WHITE FLOUR FOR DUSTING THE
BOARD

TO PREPARE THE DOUGH

Bring the 2 cups water to a boil and stir in the 7-grain cereal. Cover and continue to cook over medium heat until the water is absorbed, about 11 to 15 minutes. Remove from the heat. Cut the butter into small pieces and add it along with the honey to the hot grains. Stir to melt, then allow to cool.

After the grains have cooled to warm, pour the 1 cup warm water into a large mixing bowl and sprinkle the yeast over it. When the yeast is foamy, mix the barely warm grains into the yeast with a big wooden spoon, stirring in a continuous clockwise, circular motion, adding the 1 cup of whole wheat flour and the 1 cup all-purpose flour. Beat well after each addition. Beat this sponge in the same direction 200 more strokes. Cover the bowl with a clean tea towel and let the sponge rest about 30 to 60 minutes or until it starts to rise.

After the sponge has started to rise; in the same circular motion, beat in the salt and, one cup at a time, enough of the remaining 2 cups all-purpose flour to make a kneadable dough. The amount of flour you need to add will depend on the amount of water absorbed into the grains during the cooking process. Be sure to knead in only as much as needed to make a workable dough.

Oil your hands lightly, pour the dough out onto a clean, lightly floured board and knead, dusting the board with small amounts of white flour as needed, until smooth, about 5 to 10 minutes. Place the dough into a clean, lightly oiled bowl, turning the dough once to oil the top. Cover and let rise until doubled.

TO SHAPE AND BAKE

Lightly grease two large bread pans. Punch the dough down and knead briefly to remove any air bubbles. Divide the dough in half and shape into two loaves, rounding the tops and place seam side down into the two prepared pans. Cover with a tea towel and let rise until almost doubled. While the loaves are rising, preheat the oven to 375 degrees. Bake the loaves in the fully preheated oven for 40 to 45 minutes or until they sound hollow when tapped and the sides are golden brown. If desired, rub the tops of the loaves with butter while hot. Cool on racks to warm before slicing.

GARDEN BREAD

EGG BREAD DOUGH

YIELD: I LOAF

1¼ CUPS WARM WATER
I TABLESPOON DRY YEAST
I TABLESPOON SUGAR
2 CUPS UNBLEACHED,
  ALL-PURPOSE FLOUR
2 TABLESPOONS MELTED BUTTER
2 EGGS
1½ TEASPOONS SALT
2 TO 2½ CUPS ALL-PURPOSE FLOUR

VEGETABLES

I CUP BROCCOLI, CHOPPED
2 GREEN ONIONS, CHOPPED
½ CUP RED PEPPER, CHOPPED
I CUP GRATED CHEDDAR CHEESE

BREAD

As fresh and sweet as winds in the wheat,
Are my loaves of bread;
Each crisp and brown, when I lay them down
What a feast is spread!

For in them still are songs of the mill,
As it grinds the flour;
It's swishing wheel, where the wood folk steal,
In the twilight hour.

The noon day glow, on valleys below,
And the meadows near,
Where sunlight yields to the golden fields,
With their grain grown sere.

Dear daily staff, not sufficient, by half,
Has of you been said,
For all you ask, in your humble task,
Is the world well fed.

- Sara Wilson Middleton

TO PREPARE THE DOUGH

Pour the warm water into a large mixing bowl and sprinkle in the yeast. Beat in the sugar and the two cups of all-purpose flour until smooth. Melt the butter and, when it has cooled to warm, mix it into the dough, along with the eggs and salt. Beat in enough of the remaining all-purpose flour until the dough pulls from the sides of the bowl. Pour the dough onto a lightly floured board and knead until smooth. Place the dough into a lightly oiled bowl, turning once to oil the top. Cover with a clean tea towel and let rise until doubled.

TO ADD THE VEGETABLES

Wash and chop the vegetables and toss them with the grated cheese. When the dough has doubled in volume, knead the vegetable and cheese mixture into the dough.

TO SHAPE AND BAKE

Preheat the oven to 375 degrees. Grease 1 large or 3 small bread pans with shortening. Shape the dough into loaves and place them into the prepared pans. Let rise until almost doubled in volume. Bake in the fully preheated oven for 45 minutes to an hour, or until they sound hollow when tapped and the sides are golden.

THE ROMANTIC WINDMILL

Windmills awaken in us feelings as deep and as mystical as those with which we regard the remote and whirling stars. "The sailing ship and the windmill are both essentially romantic creations; one defying and thwarting the ungovernable fury of the sea, the other stemming the tide of the mighty wind with its frail fingers." This beautiful wind-drinking contrivance was devised to harness the forces of nature.

For centuries, millers worked to the cadence of the clicking wheel and the whirling sail. Indeed, the operation of the windmill arms was said to be much like dry land sailing. Economical mill management in those days depended upon the ability of the miller to utilize the wind to its fullest extent. A windmill was a whimsical friend and at times refused its services when it was most needed.

The gear of the sails were often made of enormous wooden teeth that were attached by an immense wooden spindle, and many had wooden cogs and machinery hewn on the spot. On days of high wind, only a few minutes were required to reduce a bushel of wheat to flour. On calm days, it might require half a day to accomplish the same result. When the mill had no grain to grind, the miller could "break" his wheel arms by lowering his upper buhr stone upon the lower. Power could be lessened by shortening the sail as one did on ships. The sails were rigged in nautical fashion and furled at night.

The outer walls were sometimes thatched with reeds, similar to those used for thatching the roofs of houses. Some boasted gabled roofs and were built of native fieldstone. Steep stairs, worn thin and hollow from the tread of the miller's feet, wound to the top, where a succession of lofty doors rose one above the other to the apex of the gable. Standing in the breast were the sacks of ground meal. Throughout the mill was the smell of broken wheat, as gently descending mealy showers made yellowish deposits on the stout oak timber beams and flooring.

While the remarkable mechanical ingenuity led to notable scientific achievements, the miller still followed his craft in a manner little different from that employed down through the ages. The miller often stood by the wheel and judged the firmness of the flour by testing it with his thumb, a time-honored device. The mills were active and prosperous in the community, patronized as they were by the entire countryside.

The windmill still continues to enchant us and retains a direct and personal charm. For centuries they were closely associated with the life, art, poetry and history of mankind, not to mention their indispensability in grinding man's grains into flour.

IMPRESSIONS OF A VISIT TO A WINDMILL

The wind is blowing from the north, the skies are laden gray.
The trees are bent before the wind, and the hedges rock and sway.
The long white sails of the old windmill are madly rushing round;
And the song of the wind through the shuttered sails makes a roaring, rushing sound.
Oh, for the life of a miller, when the winds are blowing free!
The millstone's roar and the whirl of gears are a miller's melody.
Hang a weight on the sail gear, and haul up another sack;
Let it hail or blow, let it rain or snow, there's nothing can hold us back.
Down the long spout from the millstone, the ground meal thinly flows;
And in the wooden meal trough in pyramid form it grows;
And higher it creeps and higher, and louder the north wind wails
The old mill seems it must fly away, carried by whirling sails.
Grizzled and grim is our miller, the dust has made him gray.
He fills a sack and moves it into the scale to weigh.
Take out your toll good miller, according to ancient law;
Tie up the sack and, when secure, wheel it away to store.
Grind up your corn, merry miller, 'mid the old mills rock and sway.
Gold dust mixed with flour dust, gather it while you may.
The millstone is your hourglass, the grain the sands that run.
Soon will your hour be over, your little day be done.

– R.D. Clover

CYCLE OF SEASONS

All seasons bless these rolling plains;
Springtime's quickening welcome rains,
The long midsummer's dream of heat,
Autumn's haze, gold as the wheat,
And winter's blanketing of snow
On stubbled fields that sleep below
Till spring again sounds the "all clear"
And the first new green shoots appear.
Seasons bless windmill, field and man
Keyed to nature's rhythmic span:
Sowing, reaping, reaping, sowing,
Here you can almost hear things growing!

– Ethel Jacobson

WHEAT AND BUTTER

Wheat is still. It makes no sound
As it pushes from the ground;
As it runs its slow, serene
Course in rows of tender green.

Wheat is quiet. As it grows
It only whispers what it knows.
Wheat is mute, till it is fed
To children, as a loaf of bread.
Then it is laughter; it is song;
Then it is clamor all day long.

Butter is music of wind that passes
Through blue alfalfa and supple grasses.
It is sun on meadows; it is lyric notes
Of rain and honey in clover throats.
It is the pale gold rhythmic tread
Of summer on a slice of bread.

– Ethel Romig Fuller

WHOLE WHEAT AND HONEY BRAN BREAD

YIELD: 2 LOAVES

1½ CUPS MILK

4 TABLESPOONS BUTTER

⅓ CUP HONEY

½ CUP WARM WATER

2 TABLESPOONS DRY YEAST

2 TEASPOONS SUGAR

1 CUP WHOLE WHEAT FLOUR

1 CUP BRAN FLAKES

1 CUP UNBLEACHED, ALL-PURPOSE FLOUR

1 TABLESPOON SALT

1 CUP UNBLEACHED, ALL-PURPOSE FLOUR

2 CUPS ALL-PURPOSE FLOUR FOR KNEADING

TO PREPARE THE DOUGH

Scald the milk in a small pan, then add the butter and honey to melt.

Pour the warm water into a large mixing bowl, sprinkle in the yeast and sugar and stir to dissolve. When the milk mixture has cooled to warm, and the yeast mixture is foamy, pour the milk mixture into the yeast.

Add the whole wheat flour, the bran and the 1 cup of white flour. Beat this mixture with a wooden spoon in a circular clockwise motion until smooth. Continue beating, in the same direction, 200 strokes. Let this sponge rest 30 to 60 minutes or until it starts to rise.

Beat in the salt and the next cup of white flour. Oil your hands lightly and knead the dough, flouring the board from time to time, with the remaining white flour, until smooth and elastic, about 10 minutes. Place the dough in a clean, lightly oiled bowl, turning the dough once to oil the top. Cover and let rise until doubled.

TO SHAPE AND BAKE

Punch down the dough and knead out any air bubbles. Divide the dough in half and shape into two loaves. Place the two loaves, seam side down, into two large greased loaf pans. Cover and let rise until almost doubled.

While the dough is rising preheat the oven to 375 degrees. Bake in the fully preheated oven for 40 to 45 minutes, or until the loaves sound hollow when tapped, and the tops and sides are a rich golden brown. Cool on a rack before slicing.

TOASTED NUT AND OAT BREAD

YIELD: 1 LOAF

¾ CUP RAW SUNFLOWER SEEDS
½ CUP CHOPPED PECANS
1¼ CUPS BOILING WATER
1 CUP QUICK COOKING ROLLED OATS
⅓ CUP BUTTER
¼ CUP DARK MOLASSES
2 TEASPOONS SALT
2 TABLESPOONS DRY YEAST
½ CUP WARM WATER
2 EGGS
3 CUPS UNBLEACHED, ALL-PURPOSE FLOUR
1 TO 3 CUPS ALL-PURPOSE FLOUR FOR KNEADING
1 EGG, BEATEN WITH 2 TABLESPOONS WATER

TO PREPARE THE DOUGH

Place the sunflower seeds in a small saucepan over medium heat and stir them often to toast them evenly until golden, or spread them onto a half sheet pan and roast them gently in the oven. Spread them onto a plate to cool and repeat the procedure with the pecans.

In a large bowl pour the 1¼ cups boiling water over the oats. Add the butter, molasses and salt. Stir until the butter is dissolved, then allow to cool. When the oat mixture has cooled to warm, in a small bowl, dissolve the yeast in the ½ cup of warm water. Beat the eggs into the oats and when the yeast mixture is foamy, add it in, along with the 3 cups of all-purpose flour, stirring with a wooden spoon in a circular, clockwise motion. Continue beating in the same direction 200 strokes.

Add more of the remaining all-purpose flour, ½ cup at a time, beating well after each addition, until the dough forms a ball. Flour your board and knead the dough, adding more flour if necessary, until it feels fairly firm. The oats will keep the dough moist so be sure not to over flour your board or the bread will be heavy. Place the dough into a lightly oiled bowl, turning it once to oil the top, cover and let rise until doubled.

TO SHAPE AND BAKE

Preheat the oven to 375 degrees. Lightly grease a sheet pan with shortening. After the dough has doubled in volume, punch it down and knead briefly. Shape into one nice large round loaf. Place the loaf on the prepared pan. Cover with a clean tea towel and let rise again until almost doubled. Gently and evenly brush the loaf with the beaten egg and water mixture. With a sharp knife, gently cut one 1/8 inch deep cut through the loaf. Sprinkle with the chopped nuts. Bake in the preheated oven for 40 to 50 minutes or until well browned and the loaf sounds hollow when tapped. Cool on a rack before slicing.

SHEEPHERDER LOAF

At dusk the flock was bedded down
In the shelter of the hill,
And the sheperd's fire made a cheery blaze
As night fell, hushed and chill.

From his boot the sheperd fished a knife,
From his pack he fetched his bread,
And he cut a hunk, and sat and munched,
While stars winked overhead.

Sheepherder bread! Like the harvest moon
Tawny and big and round.
And miraculously staying fresh
Till the last least crumb is downed.
Body and spirit are richly fed
With a hill, and stars, and sheeperder bread.

– Ethel Jacobson

THE OLD TIME WATER MILL

One hundred and fifty years ago, water mills dotted the banks of every fair-sized stream. The old mills were an integral part of the American scene. They were also one of the first machines invented by man to replace the sweat and toil of muscular strength with the power of nature.

Many of the old mill buildings had foundations of river rock, stone, or brick. The upper walls were built with heavy timbers and hand-hewn beams held together with huge wooden pegs. They were built strong to withstand the vibrating of the thundering gear and the rumbling of the buhrs. The barn-like weather-beaten structures grew in softness as they aged, adding to their natural charm.

The sturdy battened doors were often fitted with heavy, yet decorative, wrought iron latches. The upper part of the door opened inward, exposing a broad shelf to rest upon. When time allowed, it was the custom of the miller, in his spotless white smock, to lean over the bottom half of the door and visit with the farmers while the millstones rumbled at their faithful task.

The sound of stone on stone made a slumberous, pleasing sound, accompanied by the clack, clack, clack of the huge wheel, which creaked and groaned as its paddles revolved from the force of the stream. The swish of the running waters and the splashing sound of the stream falling over the milldam, all combined in a delightful composition, spilling their music on the air. In the summer, the shouts and laughter of boys disporting themselves in the near-by swimming hole were added to the scene.

Great trees grew before the mill porch, casting their pleasant flickering shadows over its beamed floor. Within the mill, the atmosphere was filled with fine particles of flour dust, which settled on everything and added whiteness to the miller's gray hair. When the sun shone through the few windows, it set the flour atoms dancing and floating in the golden beams of light.

TENNYSON

I love the brimming wave that swam
Thro' quiet meadows round the mill,
The sleeping pool above the dam,
The pool beneath it ever still.
The meal-sacks on the wighten'd floor,
The dark round of the dripping wheel,
The very air about the door
Made Misty with the floating meal.

With all the excitement of a pageant or play, the dusty miller and his loader were serenely busy at their prosperous task. The upper wheel turned the mill by the force of the river, while golden streams of wheat and corn were poured from above by a suspended hopper into the millstone onto the lower floor. Flour lay everywhere, between the floors, and in the nooks and crannies, where it slowly accumulated.

All grinding was paid for by toll. The hopper held a bushel, and when the grinding started a small wooden toll box, holding ⅛ of a bushel, was set to catch the miller's share. Toll was always paid in kind. The old mill's treasures included a marlin pin used in sack tying, a sack stencil, bearing the name in large capitol letters, a roll of bolting cloth prepared for use by the miller's wife, a number of stone dressing implements, and, of course, the miller's cat.

Through the heavy backwood's forest, the farmer would follow the Indian trail to the mill. Sometimes there was an overhanging cliff shelter immediately behind the mill house which afforded ample shelter for those who were waiting with their horses and mules in rain or wintry weather. Old timers recall how long rows of farm wagons lined up in front of the mill with grain consigned to the miller for grinding. It was a satisfaction to see the people coming to the flour mill with their horses loaded with grains, the fruits of their own industry, and leaving with grist ground.

This was the neighborhood exchange, frequented both by the idle and the industrious. Long, broad benches were built on raised platforms in front of the mill, their backs to the wall; three-legged stools and crude chairs, of the millwright's making during idle hours, supplemented the accommodations. The mill was not only an economical necessity, but a social asset as well. It was a rendezvous for society. Here tales were told, yarns were swapped, votes cast, the latest politics discussed, and meetings held.

From time immemorial, the old mill has been the theme of the writer, the painter, and verse-maker. The staunch old stone structure nestled next to a meandering stream, mill wheel and water engaged in a quiet dialogue of their own. What a place to drowsily loaf and dream. Is it any wonder that artists sought the mills as subjects for their sketches and paintings, and poets as inspiration for their rhymes? There is something about the old-fashioned water mill that has gripped our imagination…this relic of the days before industrialism stands in dramatic contrast to the more harried pace of our lives today and reminds us that nature holds other ways to measure a life.

> *"Take the proverb to thyne heart,*
> *Take, and hold it fast,*
> *"The mill cannot grind*
> *With the water that is past."*

The pioneer windmill and water mill are institutions that belong to our great-grandfather's day and, like them, have passed into the dim distance of time-honored past. They are both worthy of permanent preservation. The windmill and water mill and miller of the past were all a quintessential part of the economic, social, and daily life of the early settlers. Few such mills are in operation today. The old mill stream flows on now, unobstructed down its curving course.

39

AS YOUTH WILL DREAM

Across the meadow and through the wood
And over the stony hill,
How often he followed the narrow path
That led to the old red mill.
Oh the warm, sweet scent of the waking wood
As the first sweet buds uncurled,
Oh the sweet, low call of a tangled hedge,
Oh the joy that o'erflowed the world!

The bare feet followed their own sweet will
Till they reached the old mill stream,
While the little lad with tangled curls
Was lost in a golden dream.
For he dreamed of a far-off, blessed time
When his feet at last would stand
On the shining hills of his heart's desire -
In the kingdom of Grown-Up Land.

The years slipped by and the lad is one
Of the busy world of men,
But the barefoot boy and his golden dreams
Are as far apart as then.
He would give his kingdom in Grown-Up Land
For that dear old sun-kissed hill,
And the winding pathway, beset with dreams,
That led to the old red mill.

- Florence Jones Hadley

SWEDISH LIGHT RYE BREAD WITH WALNUTS

YIELD: 2 LOAVES

3 MEDIUM POTATOES	¼ CUP BUTTER
WATER TO COVER	2 TABLESPOONS SALT
1 TABLESPOON DRY YEAST	1 CUP FINELY CHOPPED WALNUTS
¾ CUP MOLASSES	2 CUPS ALL-PURPOSE FLOUR
2 CUPS RYE FLOUR	ALL-PURPOSE FLOUR FOR KNEADING
2 CUPS UNBLEACHED,	CORN MEAL FOR THE PAN
ALL-PURPOSE FLOUR	
2 TABLESPOONS CARAWAY SEEDS	

TO PREPARE THE DOUGH

Peel the potatoes and cut them into ½ inch cubes. Cover the potatoes with water in a medium-size pan and cook them until very soft. Strain and reserve the cooking liquid, adding more warm water to it until you have exactly 4 cups. Pour the water into a large mixing bowl and, when it has cooled to warm, sprinkle the yeast over it. Stir in the molasses to dissolve.

Whip the potatoes until smooth. When you are sure there are no lumps and the potatoes have cooled to warm, measure out exactly 1 cup and add it to the yeast mixture. (You may want to rice the potatoes through a strainer to be positive there are no lumps).

In a clockwise circular direction, stir in the 2 cups of rye flour, 2 cups of the all-purpose flour and the caraway seeds. Continue to beat in the same direction for 200 strokes. Let this sponge rest for 30 to 60 minutes or until it starts to rise.

Melt the butter and, when it has cooled to warm, add it, along with the salt, finely chopped walnuts and 2 more cups of white flour to the dough until well-incorporated. Knead the dough on a lightly floured board until smooth and elastic, about 10 minutes. Place the dough into a clean, lightly oiled bowl, turning once to lightly oil the top. Cover with a tea towel and let rise until doubled.

TO SHAPE AND BAKE

Preheat the oven to 375 degrees. Lightly grease a sheet pan and then dust lightly with corn meal. After the dough has doubled in volume, punch it down and knead out any air bubbles. Shape into a nice round loaf and place the loaf onto the prepared pan. Cover with a clean tea towel and let rise until almost doubled. Bake the loaf for 45 to 50 minutes, or until it sounds hollow when tapped. Cool some before slicing.

THE LOAVES

Wheat grains are shaped like loaves in miniature -
I have seen my mother shape her loaves just so,
True to the seed. Her hands, supple and sure,
Kneaded to satin smoothness mounds of dough
Whose yeasty bubbles squeaked with each down-thrust.
She shaped them then in pans long dark with wear,
And set them, whitely spread, secure from dust,
Or any vagrant chilling breath of air,
Till risen and ready for the oven's heat.
Then came the time, impatiently awaited,
With tantalizing smell of baking bread,
Until a child's imaginings were freighted
With generous crusty pieces thickly spread
With yellow butter, freshly churned and sweet,
Molded and stamped with beautiful sheaf of wheat.

- Maude Rene Princehouse

OCTOBER MORNING

This morning when I set the warm fresh loaves
Upon the sill, somehow I thought your eyes
Smiled from the arbor, but it may have been
A morning glory blue as October skies.
Was it your voice beyond the garden pool,
Or only a bird? Somehow I thought you said
In the old way, "There's nothing lovelier
Than the golden fragrance of your bread."

– Grace V. Watkins

EGG BREAD BRAID

To make the EGG BREAD BRAID pictured below, double the recipe of EGG BREAD DOUGH, located on page 28.

TO MAKE THE BRAID

Preheat the oven to 375 degrees. After the dough has doubled in volume, divide it into thirds. Roll each ⅓ into a rope on a lightly floured surface. Braid the 3 sections together; place on a lightly greased sheet-pan. Form the braid into a circle, braiding the ends together. Cover with a clean tea towel and let rise until almost doubled. Bake in the preheated oven until golden and the loaf sounds hollow when tapped.

HERB BREAD RING

To make the HERB BREAD RING pictured on the previous page, triple the EGG BREAD DOUGH recipe, located on page 28.

FRESH HERB FILLING

3-4 CLOVES OF FINELY GRATED GARLIC
2 FINELY GRATED SHALLOT
½ CUP OLIVE OIL
1 CUP CHOPPED FRESH ITALIAN PARSLEY
½ CUP CHOPPED FRESH SAGE

When the dough is rising in the bowl, finely grate the garlic and shallots into the olive oil. Chop the fresh herbs and mix them together.

Roll the dough on a lightly floured board into a rectangle. Brush the dough with the oil mixture, evenly distributing the garlic and shallots, then evenly sprinkle on the chopped fresh herbs. Roll the dough, starting with the long side, into a long even loaf. Place the loaf on a lightly greased baking sheet or one lined with parchment paper, seam side down, forming a circle. Cut 1½ inch wide cuts two-thirds into the dough all the way around. Gently turn each section slightly in a pretty pattern to expose the herbs. Let the dough rise until almost doubled. Brush with egg wash and sprinkle with sesame seeds if desired. Bake in the preheated oven until golden and the loaf sounds hollow when tapped.

THE JOLLY MILLER

In literature, the miller is always a jovial person, carefree and relaxed. He was a man of substance and of high repute, the arbitrator of local disputes, universally regarded as fair and charitable. Upright in his dealings, firm in his faith and convictions. Throughout most of pre-industrial history, the mill and the miller were symbols of joy and gaiety, abundance and prosperity.

The rhythmic movements attending the development of the science and the art of milling- the recurring beat of treading feet, the sweep of revolving sails, the turning hum of the waterwheels- drew the imagination of the miller and his audience alike. In song and rhymes, the miller and his art were celebrated as a romantic idyll.

THE MILLER OF WYE

It was a jolly miller who lived near the River Wye;
All day he ground the golden grain while the slow stream murmered by;
And as he stood beside the wheel, he sang a jolly song,
Which cheered full many a wight that passed the river road along.

And they who brought their grain unto that famous mill of old,
Laughed long and loud to hear the tales that merry miller told;
Fat paunches shook and stout ribs ached with spasms of fresh mirth;
And many vowed there never was a jollier man on earth!

The miller prospered, for the folks all came from far and near
To listen to his waggish songs, his cosmic tales to hear!
And down the hopper with the wheat went every earthly care
Of those who visited the mill and heard the miller there!

The mill's now gone; the miller, too! But folks along the Wye
Have many a jesting tale to tell of days that are gone by;
And still that jolly miller's fame lives on, and will live, though
The rich and great he knew have been forgotten long ago!

- Clarence Mansfield Lindsay

The miller was usually held to be an honest, well-meaning, and respected member of the community, always appearing with a cheery and ruddy countenance from his labor.

Old time millers were renowned for their jollity, and, throughout the industry's history, songs and rhymes extol the carefree miller, his picturesque mill, the peaceful mill stream and, quite often, his fair daughter.

"The wheel goes round,
The grist is ground,
The dusty miller's merry.
He sings all day, His work is play,
While thinking of his dearie."

Free from sorrow, free from strife,
O how blessed the miller's life!
Cheerful working through the day,
Still he laughs, and sings away.
Naught can vex him, Naught perplex him,
While there's grist to make him gay.

THE MILLER'S DAUGHTER

Women were the first millers, from Sarah grinding for Abraham to the king's milling maid of Britain. In many parts of the world, the good wife still toils at the quern. But when men took over the milling, their daughters headed straight for romance and glamour. For centuries and in every language, wherever you seek in tales and song, the miller's daughter is always, and forever "fair."

It is really quite a subject for speculation as to why the miller's daughter, and only she, was perennially and universally fair. Perhaps the running brook, the musical wheel-rush, the open casement of the miller's cottage heightened the allure. And we can all imagine the eager young farm boy, arriving at the mill gate, his farm wagon laden with sacks of wheat or corn, greeted by the "fair-faced" miller's daughter at the window. Could anything other than poetry unfold?

THE MILLER'S DAUGHTER

Here from the brow of the hill I look,
Through the lattice of boughs and leaves,
On the old gray mill with its gambrel roof,
And the moss on its rotting eaves.
I hear the chatter that jars its walls,
And rushing water's sound,
And I see the black floats rise and fall
As the wheel goes slowly round.

I rode there often when I was young,
With my grist on the horse before,
And I talked with Nelly, the miller's girl,
As I waited my turn at the door.
And while she tossed her ringlets brown,
And flirted and chatted so free,
The wheel might stop, or the wheel might go
It was all the same to me.

'Tis twenty years since I last stood
On the spot where I stand today,
And Nelly is wed, and the miller's dead,
And the mill and I are gray.
But both, till we fall into ruin and wreck,
To our fortune of toil are bound;
And the man goes and the stream flows,
And the wheel moves slowly round.

- Thomas Dunn English

BLACK BREAD

YIELD: 1 LOAF

½ CUP YELLOW CORNMEAL

3 TABLESPOONS BUTTER

¼ CUP MOLASSES

¾ CUP BOILING WATER

1 TABLESPOON YEAST

¼ CUP WARM WATER

1 EGG

2 TABLESPOONS INSTANT COFFEE

2 TABLESPOONS CAROB POWDER

1 CUP WHOLE WHEAT FLOUR

¾ CUP RYE FLOUR

2 TEASPOONS SALT

2 CUPS ALL-PURPOSE FLOUR

VEGETABLE OIL FOR YOUR HANDS

ALL-PURPOSE FLOUR FOR THE BOARD

CORNMEAL FOR DUSTING

HOMELIKE HEAVEN

The paradise of Omar Khayyam
Was wine and a loaf of bread,
And "thou" in a wilderness bower afar,
With a lover's moon overhead.

My paradise is a wilderness
Of blooms in our flower bed
And "you" there with me sharing a feast
Of coffee and home-baked bread!

- Rigmor Stone

TO PREPARE THE DOUGH

Put the cornmeal, butter, and molasses in a large bowl. Stir in the boiling water. Let cool.

In a small bowl, sprinkle the yeast over the ¼ cup warm water. When the cornmeal mixture has cooled to warm and the yeast mixture is foamy, stir the two together, along with the egg, instant coffee, carob powder, whole wheat flour and the rye flour. Beat the batter in a clockwise, circular motion for 200 strokes. Let this sponge rest until it starts to rise, about 30 to 45 minutes.

Beat in the salt and the white flour. Turn out onto a lightly floured board and with clean, lightly oiled hands knead for 10 to 15 minutes or until smooth and elastic. Place the dough into a clean, lightly oiled bowl, turning once to oil the top. Let rise until doubled.

TO SHAPE AND BAKE

Preheat the oven to 375 degrees. After the loaf has doubled in volume, punch it down and knead briefly. With lightly oiled hands, shape the dough into a nice round loaf. Place the loaf onto a lightly greased half sheet pan that has been lightly dusted with cornmeal. Cover with a clean tea towel and let rise until almost doubled.

Bake for 40 to 50 minutes, or until the loaf is browned and sounds hollow when tapped. The loaf will have better texture if allowed to cool somewhat before slicing.

ONION POPPY SEED FLAT BREAD

52

BREAD DOUGH

1 recipe of FOCACCIA DOUGH, page 54.

TOPPING

2 LARGE ONIONS, THINLY SLICED OR DICED
1 STICK BUTTER
2 TABLESPOONS POPPY SEEDS

Prepare one recipe of FOCACCIA DOUGH. While the panned dough is rising, sauté the onions in the butter until transparent. Cool some to warm, then divide the sautéed onions between the two loaves and spread them on evenly. Sprinkle on the poppy seeds. Let rest for 10 to 20 minutes, until it starts to rise.

Preheat the oven to 350 degrees. Bake for 20 to 25 minutes or until lightly golden. Cool slightly, then cut into wedges and serve.

ONION DILL BREAD

YIELD: 2 LOAVES

3 CUPS BUTTERMILK
2 TABLESPOONS MINCED ONION
2 TABLESPOONS OIL
2 CUPS SMALL-CURD COTTAGE CHEESE
4 TABLESPOONS YEAST
4 CUPS ALL-PURPOSE FLOUR
2 TABLESPOONS DILL WEED
2 TABLESPOONS SALT
2⅓ CUPS RYE FLOUR
3 TO 4 CUPS ALL-PURPOSE FLOUR
1 EGG WHITE
COARSE SALT

In a large saucepan, stir together and gently heat until warm to the touch the buttermilk, minced onion and oil. Pour the buttermilk mixture into a large mixing bowl and stir in the cottage cheese. Sprinkle the yeast over the mixture and stir to dissolve. When the yeast begins to foam, stir in 4 cups of the all-purpose flour and stir this mixture in a continuous clockwise motion for 200 strokes. Let this sponge rest for 20 minutes or until it begins to rise.

Beat in the dill weed, salt and rye flour. Beat in, one cup at a time, enough of the remaining all-purpose flour to make a soft dough. Pour the dough out onto a lightly floured board and knead until smooth and elastic, about 10 minutes. You will still see cottage cheese. Place the dough into a lightly oiled bowl, turning once to oil the top. Cover with a clean tea towel and let rise until doubled.

Preheat the oven to 375 degrees. Lightly grease a sheet pan and dust it with cornmeal. Punch down the dough and work out the air bubbles. Divide the dough in half and shape each half into 2 oblong loaves. Place the loaves onto the prepared pan. Cover the loaves with a clean tea towel and let rise until almost doubled. Brush the loaves with egg wash and sprinkle with the coarse salt. With a sharp knife, make 3 thin diagonal cuts through each loaf.

Bake for 40 to 50 minutes or until the loaves are golden and sound hollow when tapped. The bottoms should also be browned. Cool on a rack before slicing.

FOCACCIA BREAD

YIELD: 12 SMALL ROUNDS OR 2 SHEETS

1½ CUPS BOILING WATER

1 TABLESPOON BUTTER

1 TABLESPOON SUGAR

1 TABLESPOON YEAST

⅔ CUP WARM WATER

3 CUPS UNBLEACHED ALL-PURPOSE FLOUR

½ CUP POWDERED MILK

1 TABLESPOON SALT

2½-3 CUPS UNBLEACHED ALL-PURPOSE FLOUR

VEGETABLE OIL FOR THE BOWL

½ CUP OLIVE OIL

2 TEASPOONS GARLIC

4 TBS. FINELY CHOPPED FRESH ROSEMARY

4 TBS. FINELY CHOPPED FRESH SAGE

1 TEASPOON KOSHER SALT

A HOUSEKEEPER SPEAKS

These are things close to my heart:
A kitchen, and a fire to start,
A primrose on a window sill,
A view through glass of field and hill,
A yellow bowl and flour to sift.
A bright and lilting song to lift,
Above smooth shaping loaves– a heart,
Willing to do a woman's part
In a loved home, and glad, indeed,
For daily bread, and mouths to feed,
For love that lightens every task –
What more could any woman ask?
Others may choose some great career,
But mine is in my kitchen here.

– Grace Noll Crowell

Pour the 1½ cups of boiling water into a large mixing bowl. Add the butter and sugar and stir to dissolve. In a small bowl, sprinkle the yeast over the ⅔ cup warm water. In another large bowl, thoroughly mix together the 3 cups of all-purpose flour and the powdered milk. This step insures there won't be any lumps of powdered milk in the dough.

When the hot water mixture has cooled to warm and the yeast mixture is foamy, mix the 2 together in the larger bowl. Add to this the flour/milk mixture and beat with a wooden spoon in a clockwise circular direction for 200 strokes. Let this sponge rest for 30 minutes, or until it starts to rise.

Beat in the salt, and one cup at a time, enough of the remaining all-purpose flour to make a kneadable dough. Knead the dough on a lightly floured board until smooth and elastic, about 10 minutes. Place the dough into a lightly oiled bowl, turning once to oil the top. Cover with a clean tea towel and let rise until doubled.

Preheat the oven to 350 degrees. When the dough has doubled, punch it down and knead out any air bubbles. Divide the dough into 12 even pieces and on a lightly floured board roll out into rounds, or divide in half and on a lightly floured board roll the dough into 2 rectangles. Place the dough on 2 lightly greased sheet pans and allow to rise until almost doubled.

Mince or finely grate the garlic and mix it with the olive oil. Chop the fresh sage and rosemary. When the dough has almost doubled, make small indentations in the dough with your fingertips. Carefully brush the loaves with the garlic and oil mixture. Sprinkle with the chopped fresh herbs and coarse salt. Bake about 20-25 minutes or until lightly golden.

POETIC PIZZAS

YIELD: 6 SMALL OR 2 LARGE PIZZAS

1⅓ CUPS WARM WATER
1 TABLESPOON YEAST
2 CUPS ALL-PURPOSE FLOUR
1 TEASPOON SALT
¼ CUP OLIVE OIL
1¾ CUPS ALL-PURPOSE FLOUR
FLOUR FOR KNEADING
CORNMEAL FOR DUSTING THE PAN
¼ CUP OLIVE OIL
1 TEASPOON FINELY GRATED FRESH GARLIC

TOPPING SUGGESTIONS

ITALIAN TOMATOES
GREEN PEPPER
RED PEPPER
PURPLE ONION
CRUMBLED FETA CHEESE
FRESH GRATED MOZZARELLA
FRESH BASIL LEAVES
FRESH OREGANO

BAKING DAY

"I want to write a poem,"
I told myself that day.
Then I phoned Rosemary's teacher,
And cleared the crumbs away.

I set my sponge, I shined my pans,
I wound the kitchen clock,
And darned a fine new pattern
On a devastated sock!

Then I had to knead the dough,
And fold my laundry down,
And read a bit of history
For club, next day, in town.

At dusk I sighed, "My poem-"
But my hungry family said,
"You've made five gorgeous verses
In those perfect loaves of bread!"

- Anna Manley Pearson

Pour the warm water into a large bowl and sprinkle in the yeast. When the yeast is foamy, add the 2 cups flour and stir with a wooden spoon in a continuous clockwise, circular motion for 200 strokes. Allow this mixture to rise for 10 minutes.

Stir in the salt, ¼ cup olive oil and the remaining 1¾ cups flour until smooth. Pour the dough out onto a lightly floured board and knead about 10 minutes or until smooth and elastic. Place the dough into a lightly oiled bowl and turn once to lightly oil the top. Let rise until almost doubled.

Dust a sheet pan with cornmeal. Divide the dough and shape into 6 small or 2 large pizzas and let them rise on the prepared sheet pan until almost doubled. Preheat the oven to 350 degrees.

Finely grate the garlic and mix it with the remaining ¼ cup olive oil. Brush the tops lightly with the olive oil mixture and decorate with your favorite grated cheeses and thinly sliced and diced fresh vegetables and herbs.

Bake in the fully preheated oven for 35 to 45 minutes, or until the edges are golden and the bottom is slightly browned.

BREAD THAT FEEDS THE SOUL

It's made into loaves, great, crispy, browned ones –
Long and skinny ones, fat and round ones,
Pounded to sheets as thin as paper,
Rolled into sticks like a slender taper,
Braided, twisted, plain or laced
With nuts and fruits to the queen's own taste –
But in any land from pole to pole
It's Bread, Bread, Bread, that feeds the soul!

– Ethel Jacobson

THE MILLING REVOLUTION

The miller worked at mastering his craft by choosing his millstones more selectively, and the "dressing" of the millstones became a special art. Few, if any real changes, however, were made in the actual milling process, which remained virtually unchanged in 1800 from what it had been in the 4th century.

The world needed more flour, and yet the pace of the leisurely millstone was as unhurried as if nothing more than a few hundred villagers were dependent upon its activity. It was inevitable that the merchant mills would gradually encroach upon and replace our old friend, the gristmill.

The patenting of the steam engine by James Watt in 1769 and the application of the steam engine to the locomotive by George Stephenson in 1829 are the dates which mark the real beginning of modern flour milling. With steam power, a flour mill of almost any size could be built in almost any location, enabling the miller to escape the limitations of water and wind power and to increase the capacity of his mill to the full extent of his selling ability.

From 1835 to 1850, there was an enormous boom in the railway industry; tracks were laid down furiously across the United States and in Europe. This vastly enlarged the area from which the miller could draw his wheat, and the problem of transporting flour was solved. The small country miller was at last beginning to be dislodged from the position he had held for 15 centuries. Extended trade awaited him.

A revolution was beginning.

It was Watt himself who was largely responsible for the first practical application of steam power to flour milling. In 1773, he formed a company in London to build a large flour mill with power provided by engines built by himself and Boulton, his partner. The mill was built on the bank of the Thames near the southeastern end of Blackfriars' Bridge and began operation in 1786. It was equipped with 20 pairs of millstones, each 4½ feet in diameter, and each pair capable of grinding 10 bushels of wheat an hour. The mill was known as the Albion Mill. Due to its success, it was not long before steam-driven mills began to appear at various places both in England and on the continent.

Another revolution in the style, versus the technology of milling, was the development of "high" grinding. In this process, the reduction of grain is accomplished by successive partial grindings instead of by a single operation. Gradual reduction milling had been in use for some time in France, certainly since the middle of the 18th century. But it was not until the early 19th century that Austrian mills demonstrated the commercial superiority of "high" over "low" grinding. It was from the work of these stone mills, in fact, that Austrian flour won its initial reputation.

The adaptation of high grinding to greater commercial use was enormously significant. Gradual reduction meant that, after each grinding, the middlings, as they later were called, were resifted to eliminate waste, and this process resulted in considerably more flour from every bushel of wheat. The milling business prospered, and the demand for its products widened.

THE OLD STONE MILL

Just where the river road winds and curves
At the foot of the stony hill,
A little white bridge stands sentinel
Over an old stone mill.
The pigeons strut on the mossy roof
Where the sunset warmest lies,
And in and out through the open door
The nesting swallow flies.

The old millstones are covered with dust
And the water wheel is still;
The grass grows over the old-time road
And up to the worn doorsill,
Where once the miller in a powdered suit
Would stand, as each load came in,
And welcomed all with a cheer voice
That rang out above the din.

I followed the old road down the hill
And stand in the open door;
I wait for a face and a ringing laugh,
But the miller comes no more.
The old millstones are covered with dust
And the water wheel is still,
But memories of those vanished days
Hallow the old stone mill.

- Florence Jones Hadley

59

THE ROLLER MILL

Many of the millers felt a pang of deep and genuine regret when their millstones, the faithful servants of many years standing, were set aside. But progress was the order of the day, and those who did not keep step were overwhelmed by the change and their enterprises perished.

There is a question even among millers of today, where the invention of the roller mill actually took place. The design was of French origin. In 1588, or thereabouts, Augustino Ramelli, a military engineer in the service of Henry III of France, published a design for a flour mill which employed the corrugated iron roll. Bocklerum's "Theatrum Machinarum," published in 1662, also contained a design for a roller mill, wherein the single roll revolved against a fixed base extending through a quarter circle. Hazlitt describes a sort of roller mill in his book on husbandry, published in 1651, and Isaac Wilkinson actually took out a patent for a roller mill, using "a new sort of cast metallic rolls," in 1753. As applied to practical flour milling, however, nothing was done with the roller process until the second quarter of the 19th century.

The reason for the late development of roller milling was not, as is generally assumed, the failure of the milling engineers to recognize the superiority of rolls over millstones. It was purely a mechanical problem: inadequate power transmission. Water or wind power might turn a millstone 4 feet in diameter at a sufficient rate of speed, but without either elaborate gearing or a satisfactory system of rope, belt, or chain drive, a roller (with a diameter of only a few inches) could not develop enough speed to secure satisfactory results.

Until 1785, when John Rennie introduced metal gears in the equipment of the Albion Mills, gears and shafting were almost invariably made of wood; hence, they were clumsy, inefficient and liable to wear and breakage. The introduction of roller milling on any large scale awaited the development of a form of power capable of driving the rolls at the requisite rate of speed.

For some years, it had been known that the millers of Budapest, Hungary, were making flour of a very superior quality by a different process using rolls of porcelain, or perhaps of steel, instead of or possibly in addition to millstones. This was a secret process which they guarded jealously.

In 1871, a machine called the purifier came into use in America. The discovery and adaptation of the purifier did not in the least disturb the long-continued reign of the millstone as the method of grinding. The ponderous and faithful upper and lower buhrs still rumbled slowly at their task. The purifier improved the quality of the flour, but did not increase the pace at which flour was made.

American mill builders had experimented with porcelain rolls, imported from Zurich, but in 1878 they were not considered practical for American use. To meet the demands of his business, the American miller was determined to put to the test the new method of grinding, and in 1879 the first complete automatic roller mill in the world was built. Steel rolls were substituted for millstones. It was found that the rolls could produce flour as well as the millstones and at a much faster pace.

Together, the purifier and the rolls, which became known worldwide as the "Hungarian process," revolutionized the milling industry completely. The capacity of the mills was enormously increased, and the economic advantage of the rolls was demonstrated in increased profits. Centralization of plants became essential to success, and the large flour mills rapidly absorbed the business of the smaller ones which could not compete with them. It was just a question of time, and a short amount of time at that, before the fate of the old gristmill was sealed and the ancient millstone consigned to history.

The populations of the great centers were steadily increasing, demanding that more and larger mills be constructed to grind flour for them. The American mill building and mill furnishing trade, which had been practically dormant for generations, suddenly awoke to a feverish activity. New machines of all kinds, designed to fit into the revolutionized method of making flour, were invented, patented, and vigorously advocated by their inventors. Then followed a building and remodeling of the flour mills such as the world has never known, before or since, and will probably never know again. Many mills were rebuilt according to the latest ideas, only to be remodeled within a year according to a still more recent notion.

Today the modern flour mill is one of the most fascinating examples of modern ingenuity and inventive genius to be found anywhere. Where the miller of yesterday formerly worked by rule of thumb, he now has the council of the chemist, who furnishes him with all the important information, from the check points throughout the entire process. The mill implements many types of technology, from skills handed down through the ages to the most current science available. Of even greater importance however, is the fact that modern technology allows the miller to keep up with the world's ever-growing demand for wheat.

LORD, GIVE US BREAD

I had forgotten, as the young forget,
The steep roof sloping to the weathered walls,
Oak beams enveloped in a dusty cloak,
And narrow windows where the sunlight falls.

I had forgotten how my father's voice,
Even and steady as the turning wheel,
Lifted above the swiftly whirling stones:
"Good flour," he'd say, "you know it by the feel."

I had forgotten this, and much besides:
White gulls alert, a boy's enchanted hour,
The millwheel turning to the river's thrust,
My father's thankful voice, "Good wheat, good flour."

Moments, he'd linger at the open door:
"The yield this year is fine. Good flour, good bread.
Remember this: the world need never starve
While men resow their fields of wheat, gold-red."

Remembering, I saw the wheat fields lie
In promise and fulfillment, calling still
For men to look beneath the husks of greed,
For men to move in wisdom through a mill.

- Sadie Fuller Seagrave

PART TWO

CLASSIC RECIPES FOR HOME BAKING DEDICATED TO THE FLOUR MILLING INDUSTRY OF AMERICA

OUR PAST MILLENNIUM, A DEDICATION

Flour mills in the early 1900's were primarily engaged in supplying the household flour trade with the growing baking business accounting for 10 to 15 percent of the sales. Many had a trade within, and to some extent, outside their home communities. Some had connections in metropolitan markets but few had outlets overseas. Today's commercial bakeries use more than three-fourths of the miller's daily output with America being the largest producer of wheat in the world. Flour milled in the United States today is shipped to all parts of the world to feed the hungry nations.

The conversion of flour milling from pioneer establishments that served small communities into today's great commercial enterprises, is one of the true romances of industrial history. In the last 200 years, the flour milling industry has advanced more technologically then in all previous years combined. With all the modern developments of an ancient trade, beginning with the discovery of the middlings purifier and the substitution of the rolls for the millstone, the passing of the gristmill and the coming of the merchant mill, and still later, the unification of individual mills into groups of mills under one central control, were logical, progressive and providential steps in making for the greatest good to the greatest number. Had not the gristmill and the millstone been succeeded by the merchant mill and the rolls, the world would have been hard put to find sufficient bread with which to satisfy its hunger.

In the middle of the 1800's, there were 25,000 small grist mills that dotted the banks of every fair-sized stream. By the 1900's, only 13,000 mills criss-crossed the United States. Today, as we enter our new millennium, our nation has approximately 100 flour milling companies. These same milling companies were here throughout the last century and have contributed greatly to the industry's present importance.

This book is a dedication to the many that have made possible this last millennium of progress and achievement in the flour milling industry and to all the flour millers and milling companies that have come and gone.

The old gristmill and windmill inevitably had to make way for man's growing needs. Commemorated both in legend and in art, they deserve preservation and a place among the important mileposts of history. The grist miller of old, with his white smock, powdery hair, and cheerful countenance may be gone from sight, but his spirit lives in the hearts of romantics everywhere.

WINGS OVER GRAIN

Today when the sun shone after rain,
I saw the Guardian Angel of Grain;
Summer, herself...I saw pinions unfold
Over the fields- such a shimmer of gold!
And, of truth, felt her breath, windy-warm, sweet,
As she shook pollen down on stigmas of wheat;
As she shook pollen down on my heart, too,
When faith was conceived, and I knew, I knew
As sure as I glimpsed irradiance, there
Would be bread for me, with loaves to share...
Still even more: given flour's release,
Troubled nations were nearer peace,
And all because today after rain,
Mist, sun-burnished, seemed wings over grain.

- Ethel Romig Fuller

A LIST OF THE UNITED STATES MILLING COMPANIES THAT WILL BE TAKING US INTO THE NEW MILLENNIUM

ADM MILLING COMPANY
AGWAY COUNTY PRODUCTS GROUP
ALLEN BROTHERS MILLING CO.
AMHERST MILLING CO., INC.
ARROWHEAD MILLS, INC.
ASHLAND MILLING CO.
THE ATTALA CO.
BARTLETT MILLING CO.
BAY STATE MILLING COMPANY
THE BERKETT MILLS
BIG J MILLING & ELEVATOR CO.
BIG SPRING MILL, INC.
BRANDT MILLS, INC.
BRANDT'S FLOUR MILL, INC.
BROOKNEAL MILLING CO., INC.
F.M. BROWN'S SONS, INC.
CALIFORNIA MILLING COMPANY
CAPITOL MILLING COMPANY
CARGILL FOODS FLOUR MILLING
CEREAL FOOD PROCESSORS, INC.
CHAMPLAIN VALLEY MILLING CORP.
CHELSEA MILLING CO.
CLIFTON MILL CO.
CLOVER HILL MILLING CO.
CONAGRA FLOUR MILLING COMPANY
CORTEZ MILLING CO.
CRESCENT MILLS
CURRY FLOUR MILLS, INC.
DESERET MILLS & ELEVATORS
EDWARDS MILL
FISHER MILLS, INC.
GENERAL MILLS, INC.
GILT EDGE FLOUR MILLS, INC.
GREENFIELD MILLS, INC.
GREENWOOD ROLLER MILLS
HARVEST STATES MILLING
HEARN & RAWLINS, INC.
HEARTLAND WHEAT GROWERS L.P.
HFM
HODGSON MILL, INC.
HOMESTEAD MILLS
HOPKINSVILLE MILLING CO.
HUMBOLDT GRAIN & FLOUR CO.
JEWEL EVANS FAMILY FOODS, INC.
KANSAS STATE UNIVERSITY
KERRY, INC.
KEYNES BROTHERS
KING MILLING CO.
KNAPPEN MILLING CO.

LACY MILLING COMPANY
LAKESIDE MILLS, INC.
LEHI ROLLER MILLS CO., INC.
LOG CITY MILLING
MEACHAM MILLS
THE MENNEL MILLING CO.
THE MENNEL MILLING CO. OF VIRGINIA
MIDSTATE MILLS, INC.
MIDWEST GRAIN PRODUCTS, INC.
MILLER MILLING
MILNER MILLING, INC.
MONTANA FLOUR & GRAIN
THE MORRISON MILLING CO.
NABISCO BRANDS, INC.
NABISCO MILLING
H. NAGEL & SON CO.
NEW HOPE MILLS
C.O. NOLT & SON, INC.
NORTH DAKOTA MILL & ELEVATOR
NORTHERN CROPS INSTITUTE
NORTH STATE MILLING CO., INC.
NUNN MILLING CO., INC.
ORLINDA MILLING CO., INC.
PANHANDLE MILLING CO.
PENDLETON FLOUR MILLS
PIONEER FLOUR MILLS
PURITY FOODS, INC.
ROCKY MOUNTAIN FLOUR MILLING
SANFORD MILLING CO., INC.
SCOTT'S AUBURN MILLS, INC.
SHAWNEE MILLING CO.
SIEMER MILLING CO.
SNAVELY'S MILL, INC.
SOUTHEASTERN MILLS, INC.
STAFFORD COUNTY FLOUR MILLS CO.
STAR OF THE WEST MILLING CO.
STONE GROUND MILLS
TERMINAL FLOUR MILLS
TUTHILLTOWM GRIST MILL
THE WALL-ROGALSKY MILLING CO.
WAUNETA ROLLER MILLS, INC.
WEISENBERGER MILLS, INC.
H.R. WENTZEL SONS, INC.
WHEATLAND MILLING, INC.
WHITE LILY FOODS CO.
WILKINS-ROGERS, INC.
THE WILLIAMS BROTHERS CO.
WILSON'S CORN PRODUCTS, INC.
THE QUAKER OATS CO.

THANKSGIVING

For green fields where the prodigal sun squanders
For precious gold of his life giving rays,
For soft winds and each billowy cloud that wanders
Freighted with rain for thirsty summer days;
For yellow grain that ripens while we sleep,
For bursting granaries that recieve the hoard
Of Autumn's gold, for those who sow and reap,
For seedtime and harvest we thank Thee, Lord.

For nature's harnessed forces where the mill
Grinds out the white dust that is hunger's foe
We thank Thee, and for all who toil until
The brown loaf issues from the oven's glow.
When thankful praise for all good things is said,
Lord, may we not forget our daily bread.

John H. Knox

CHAPTER ONE

SCONES AND OTHER BREAKFAST ITEMS

DECICATED TO THE FISHER MILLS INC.

EST. 1911

FISHER MILLS INC.

Fisher Mills, Inc., formerly Fisher Flouring Mills Co., located in Seattle, Washington, is the largest independently-owned mill in the United States. Oliver William Fisher founded the business dynasty which bears his name.

He was born in a log cabin in Wheelersburg, Ohio, on September 2nd, 1842, the fourth of five sons of Peter and Lucretia Fisher. His father died when he was eight, which forced him and his brothers to abandon school and work to support their family. By the age of 12, Oliver William was apprenticed to learn the trade of miller, which for years he preferred to any other occupation. He was lithe and strong, and from early boyhood, accustomed to hard work.

In London, Ontario, he became an apprentice to a grist miller. Later, he and his new bride, Euphemia Robinson, moved to Humansville, Missouri, where he acquired a combination saw/grist mill, dividing the week between the two businesses. When Oliver William operated the grist mill, he worked 24 hours a day. At night, he would pour two to three broad bags of grain into the mill, then sleep up against the mill when it was operating, being awakened by the difference in sound when the grist had run through. He would then refill the mill and bag the flour.

Late in 1881, Oliver William sold or traded his Humansville holdings for a larger mill at Boliver, the seat of Poke County, and he then had his first experience operating a merchant mill. A merchant mill was a mill large enough to produce flour for sale, whereas a grist mill usually made flour for those who brought grist to the mill.

Through the years, O. W., as he had become affectionately known, acquired considerable acumen and ability. He was strong-minded and positive, and had become a leader among men. He had the indefinable quality called "sound business judgment".

O. W. had learned the art of flour milling on stone buhrs, which for thousands of years had been the conventional method of crushing wheat and milling flour. In the late 1870's, the stones were supplanted by corrugated steel rolls, which had first come to America from Hungary. By then, too, the middlings purifier had been perfected, which made it possible to separate the flour streams more precisely than in the past. O. W. marveled at these technological improvements and, unlike many old-timers, did not oppose them.

The Pacific Northwest, due to its heavy rainfall, is noted for wheat with a low protein content. The wheat easily draws moisture from the rain-soaked earth, creating a soft flour when it is ground. Ideal for cake and pastry baking, the flour was soon found by the early settlers to be unsuitable for baking bread.

The wheat grown in the drier climate on the eastern side of the Cascade Mountains contains a higher protein content, and it was realized that, if the Northwest could gain access, it would inevitably become an important milling center. The West Shore, a Portland magazine, said in June 1884: "There is an industry not at present represented in Seattle but which when a railroad is constructed across the Cascades will surely become an important one. With an abundance of coast close to the cities and with the harbors full of vessels of the grain fleet, great milling interest must inevitably spring up here and the shipments of grain and flour will assume large proportions."

Late in the decade James H. Hill began expanding his Great Northern Line westward. Rumors that Seattle would be the likely terminus fueled a population boom and an acceleration of real estate values.

Realizing that this was a location where the world was his market, O. W. Fisher entered into a partnership with his five sons to create the Fisher Flouring Mill Co. In 1910 on Harbor Island near the Port, the family installed the largest mill ever built in Seattle. The mill was first equipped with several sets of stones that were later replaced by the roller process. They milled and delivered their first flour in April of 1911. Much of the mills original equipment is still in use. The mill runs twenty four hours a day, six days a week.

O. W. and Euphemia Robinson-Fisher reared a family whose members gained distinction through their own efforts and greatly expanded their father's business realm. In addition to their domestic sales, the Fisher Flour Mill ships flour directly to Hawaii, Alaska, Central and South America, and the Orient.

PROPER BAKING PROCEDURES
SCONES AND OTHER BREAKFAST ITEMS

PREHEATING THE OVEN

Scones and biscuits only take minutes to prepare, so start preheating the oven before you start the dough. This step allows the scones to be placed in the oven immediately after being cut and panned, which helps any activated ingredients maintain their strength. The leavening agents also need the direct high heat in order to give the best performance in the oven.

PREPARING THE PANS

Line a half-sheet of full-sheet pan (depending on the size of your oven) with parchment paper or use shortening to lightly grease the pan. Parchment paper can be purchased at local cooking stores and gives most everything baked on sheet pans a more professional appearance. It is well worth the expense.

CUTTING IN THE BUTTER

For lighter scones and biscuits, be sure the butter is cold. Cut it into the dry mixture with either a pastry cutter, 2 knives, or cut into small pieces and mix in a mixer on low speed, until it resembles coarse meal. The small butter pieces in the dough will melt during the baking process, separating the dough into layers, making the scones and biscuits tender and flaky.

WORKING WITH THE LEAVENING AGENTS

Baking powder is activated by heat. When mixed with liquid and heated, it produces a carbon dioxide gas, which makes the product rise. Baking soda is activated by acids and is used in recipes which contain ingredients such as buttermilk or sour cream. When the baking soda comes in contact with the necessary acid, it rapidly releases a carbon dioxide gas. Therefore, working with the dough quickly, helps to retain the gas, allowing more volume in the finished product.

MIXING AND HANDLING OF THE DOUGH

Scones and biscuits call for a flaky texture. Scrape the dough out of the bowl onto a lightly floured board and work with it briefly just to give it form. Overworking the dough will develop the gluten, which hinders volume in leavened goods.

CUTTING THE SHAPES

When cutting the shapes, space the cuts as close as possible so that there is little or no leftover dough. Each time the leftover dough is reworked, it further develops the gluten.

COOLING AND STORING

Remove the hot scones and biscuits from the sheet pan and place them on a rack to cool. Serve them warm. Any leftover scones and biscuits should be cooled completely, then wrapped in foil to be gently reheated to serve at a later time.

THE MAJESTY OF FLOUR

Some housewives find more beauty in
A loaf of bread, well browned,
Than others find in pageantries
Of art and scenes renowned.

To them it represents the score
Of perfect kitchen power,
Backed by the quality and strength
Of honest, well milled flour.

-Ivan Moyer Thomas

SUNFLOWER OATMEAL SCONES

YIELD: 8 TO 12 SCONES

¾ CUP DICED, DRIED PINEAPPLE
¾ CUP DICED, DRIED APRICOTS
¼ CUP APPLE JUICE
1¼ CUPS ROLLED OATS
½ CUP PLUS 2 TABLESPOONS RAW,
   SHELLED SUNFLOWER SEEDS
3 CUPS ALL-PURPOSE FLOUR
3 TABLESPOONS BAKING POWDER
1 TEASPOON SALT
5 TABLESPOONS SUGAR
1 CUP (2 STICKS) COLD BUTTER,
   CUT INTO SMALL PIECES
4 EGGS
⅔ CUP COLD BUTTERMILK
ZEST OF ½ LEMON

Preheat the oven to 350 degrees. Lightly grease a sheet pan with shortening or line it with parchment paper.

TO PREPARE THE DOUGH

In a small bowl, combine the diced pineapple and apricots. Add the apple juice and stir to coat the fruit. Leave the mixture to soak while you prepare the rest of the ingredients.

In a blender or food processor whirl the oats briefly until they resemble coarse meal. The oats should now measure approximately 1 cup. Repeat the process with the sunflower seeds, until they too, look like course meal. In a large bowl, combine the ground oats and sunflower seeds and to this mixture add the flour, baking powder, salt and sugar. Toss or stir gently to mix thoroughly.

Add the cold butter pieces to the dry ingredients. With a pastry cutter, or 2 knives, cut them into the mixture until it resembles coarse meal.

Beat the eggs with the buttermilk and fresh lemon zest. Stir in the diced fruit mixture. Pour this mixture into the dry ingredients and stir with a fork until the mixture follows the fork around the bowl. Pour the dough out onto a lightly floured board and knead briefly, just to bind.

TO PAN AND BAKE

Pat the dough into a 10-inch circle and place it onto the prepared pan. Score the dough into 8 to 12 wedges. Bake in the fully preheated oven for 20 to 25 minutes or until lightly golden. Cool slightly before breaking into wedges.

BREAD OF LIFE

The sky is just an old blue sieve,
With which, like any good housewife,
The Maker mixes Bread of Life,
Which helps the hungry world to live.

He sifts the sun and rain and snow
With infinite, unerring art,
And peace and pain in measured part,
To make the sacramental dough.

And then, that rich ingredient,
The starshine gives exotic taste,
And moonlight pours with wondrous waste,
Just where the ancient sieve is rent!

- Earl Bigalow Brown

CHERRY CREAM SCONES

YIELD: 12 SCONES

¾ CUP DRIED, RED SOUR PITTED CHERRIES
   OR ROYAL INN CHERRIES
BOILING WATER TO COVER
2 CUPS UNBLEACHED ALL-PURPOSE FLOUR
¼ CUP SUGAR
1 TABLESPOON BAKING POWDER
½ TEASPOON SALT
1¼ CUPS HEAVY CREAM
2 TABLESPOONS ORANGE OR LEMON ZEST
1½ TABLESPOONS MELTED BUTTER

Preheat the oven to 425 degrees.

Lightly grease a sheet pan or line it with parchment paper.

NOSTALGIA

In the early hours of morning,
Often comes a strange unrest,
A sad sweet longing for the things
In childhood loved the best.

I remember well the fragrance
Of the clover fields in May,
Of rich, dark soil but lightly turned,
The scent of dew moist hay.

But there's a fonder memory,
To yearning ever wed,
When I seem to sense the fragrance
Of our mother's home made bread.

- Mary Timmons

TO PREPARE THE DOUGH

In a small bowl, cover the cherries with boiling water to plump for 5 minutes. Drain and pat dry on paper towels.

In a large bowl whisk together the flour, sugar, baking powder and salt. Measure the cream into a small bowl, stir in the drained cherries and the orange or lemon zest. Pour this mixture into the flour mixture and stir until the dough starts to mass in the center of the bowl. On a lightly floured board, knead the dough a few times to help distribute the cherries.

TO PAN AND BAKE

Pat the dough into a 10 inch circle and place it onto the prepared pan. Brush the dough with the melted butter and score into 12 wedges. Bake the scones in the fully preheated oven for 12 minutes, or until lightly browned and the center is firm to the touch. Let cool slightly before separating.

TEA SCONES WITH GOLDEN RAISINS

YIELD: 10 TO 12 SCONES

4 CUPS FLOUR
3 TABLESPOONS BAKING POWDER
1 TEASPOON SALT
5 TABLESPOONS SUGAR
1 CUP (2 STICKS) COLD BUTTER
1½ CUPS GOLDEN RAISINS
4 EGGS
⅔ CUP COLD BUTTERMILK

EGG WASH

1 EGG WHITE, BEATEN
2 TABLESPOONS COLD WATER
SUGAR FOR SPRINKLING

Preheat the oven to 350 degrees.

TO PREPARE THE DOUGH

Into a large mixing bowl, lightly sift together the flour, baking powder, salt and sugar. Cut the cold butter into small pieces and add it to the flour mixture. Using a pastry cutter, cut the butter into the flour mixture until it resembles coarse meal. Toss in the golden raisins.

Beat together the eggs and the buttermilk and pour this mixture into the flour mixture. Mix gently, scraping the bottom of the bowl until the mixture begins to follow the spoon around the bowl. Scrape the dough out of the bowl onto a lightly floured board and knead very briefly, only enough to bind.

TO PAN

Pat the scone dough into a square 1 inch high. Cut the dough into 2 inch diamonds, or cut it with a decorative cutter and place them onto a half sheet pan lined with parchment paper or onto an ungreased cookie sheet.

TO PREPARE THE EGG WASH AND BAKE

Beat the egg white with the cold water and brush the scones lightly. Sprinkle them with sugar, and bake the scones in the fully preheated oven for 12 minutes, or until they start to turn golden.

SOMETHING IN A WOMAN

Something in a woman
Loves a curtain ruffled,
Candle-light, and rugs
Braided, and muffled
Sound of the kettles singing:
Something loves a red
Flower in a window,
And the scent of bread,
New-baked, about the house
Oh, and silver gleaming...
Something in these things
Sets a woman dreaming!

- Elaine V. Emans

AUNTIE'S TENDER BUTTERMILK BISCUITS

YIELD: 10 BISCUITS

2 CUPS UNSIFTED,
    ALL PURPOSE FLOUR
1 TABLESPOON BAKING POWDER
½ TEASPOON BAKING SODA
¼ TEASPOON SALT
1 TABLESPOON SUGAR
½ CUP (4 OUNCES) COLD BUTTER
1 CUP COLD BUTTERMILK

Preheat the oven to 375 degrees.

SECOND PRIZE

Whatever the season, whatever the weather,
Granddad and biscuits belonged together.
In March or December, in August or May
He insisted that Grandmother place an array
Of biscuits in front of him three times a day.

Her warnings were frequent, her warnings were acid,
But Granddad continued unruffled amd placid
In spite of her somber predictions that she,
Whose pattern of diet was hot-biscuit- free,
Would survive by at least ten years longer than he.

When I set Granddads's biscuits before him this noon,
He served himself jam with a generous spoon,
Then wistfully smiling, he told me, "It's clear
That all factors considered, your biscuits are near
As light as I had when your Grandma was here."

- Grace V. Watkins

TO PREPARE THE DOUGH

In a large bowl, mix together the flour, baking powder, baking soda, salt and sugar. Cut the cold butter into small pieces and add it to the flour mixture. Using a pastry cutter, cut it into the flour mixture until it resembles coarse meal.

Add the buttermilk and mix gently, scraping the bottom of the bowl until the dough starts to follow the fork around the bowl. To keep the biscuits light and fluffy be sure not to over-mix. Turn the dough out onto a lightly floured board and knead slightly to bind.

TO PAN

Lightly flour the board again and roll the dough into an 8-inch circle about 1 inch high. Cut the dough into rounds with a 2-inch biscuit cutter and place them on a lightly greased sheet pan or one lined with parchment paper.

TO BAKE

Bake in the fully preheated 375 degree oven for 12 to 15 minutes, or until the biscuit tops are lightly golden.

GRANDPA'S BUTTERMILK CLOUDS

YIELD: 8 TO 10 PANCAKES

1⅔ CUPS BUTTERMILK
1 TABLESPOON CIDER VINEGAR
3 TABLESPOONS BUTTER
3 LARGE EGGS, SEPARATED
1½ CUPS ALL-PURPOSE FLOUR
1 TEASPOON BAKING POWDER
1 TEASPOON BAKING SODA
⅓ TEASPOON SALT
1 TABLESPOON SUGAR
OIL FOR SKILLET

PANCAKE WORSHIP

Griddle cakes, flannel cakes,
Call them what you will,
But pile them in a hearty stack
And let me eat my fill.
Flapjacks, crepe suzette,
To you my lyre is strumming.
And, to the cook, a hint:
Keep 'em hot and keep'em coming!

– Ethel Jacobson

TO PREPARE THE BATTER

In a small bowl, stir together the buttermilk and cider vinegar and let stand.

Start preheating a large heavy ungreased skillet on medium heat while you prepare the batter. This helps the pan to attain uniform heat distribution. Melt the butter in a small pan over low heat.

Beat the egg yolks in a large bowl until light. Add the buttermilk and cider vinegar mixture.

Sift together the flour, baking powder, baking soda, salt and sugar. Add the flour mixture to the buttermilk mixture and beat only slightly to blend.

Beat the egg whites until stiff, but not dry and fold them into the batter, along with the melted butter.

TO COOK

Lightly grease the preheated skillet. Drop the batter by large rounded spoonfuls onto the hot skillet and cook the pancakes until the entire surface is covered with air bubbles; turn and cook the other side until golden.

SUNDAY EVENING WAFFLES

83

YIELD: 4 LARGE WAFFLES

6 TABLESPOONS BUTTER, MELTED
2 CUPS ALL-PURPOSE FLOUR
2 TEASPOONS BAKING POWDER
1 TEASPOON BAKING SODA
½ TEASPOON SALT
2 CUPS BUTTERMILK
2 EGGS

TO PREHEAT THE WAFFLE IRON

Start preheating the waffle iron before you start the batter so that it has enough time to come up to the correct temperature before you pour in the batter. The light should go out on the lid when it is hot enough.

TO PREPARE THE BATTER

In a small pan, slowly melt the butter.

In a large bowl, stir together the flour, baking powder, baking soda and salt. In another bowl, whisk together the buttermilk, eggs and melted butter. Add the buttermilk mixture to the dry ingredients and beat until almost smooth.

TO BAKE

Pour some of the batter onto the hot iron, leaving room for the waffle to spread as it bakes. The waffle is baked when the steam stops escaping from the lid, or when the waffle is golden brown.

SUNDAY EVENING WAFFLES

The fire is blazing on the bricks,
The cloth is laid, the candles shine,
Now is the witching time to mix
A social batter, smooth and fine.

From flowered bowl and silver spoon,
Its creamy richness dribbles down
On sizzling steel, transforming soon
Each disc to crisp delicious brown.

There must be butter firm and sweet,
And syrup in a crystal cup;
And every guest must rise replete,
And come next Sunday night to sup.

- Margaret Ashmun

SYRUP SEASON

When nights are bright with crackling cold
But days are warming with the sun
The woodlots feel the stir of spring
And maple sap begins to run.

That was the time our mother took
To ladle out on every plate
Her syrup-season extra treat.
How we loved it! How we ate!

I wish I had one here right now;
I'd sneer at every calorie
To have a fritter, hot and brown,
Swimming in a syrup sea.

- Eloise Wade Hackett

SUNLIT POPOVERS

85

YIELD: 6 POPOVERS

2 EGGS, BEATEN
1 CUP MILK
1 TABLESPOON COOKING OIL
1 CUP ALL-PURPOSE FLOUR
½ TEASPOON SALT

MARINATED FRUITS

2 CUPS FRESH SLICED PEACHES
2 CUPS FRESH SLICED NECTARINES
1 CUP FRESH BLUEBERRIES
GRAND MARNIER
POWDERED SUGAR FOR DUSTING

Clean and slice all fresh fruit into a bowl. Add the berries and pour the Grand Marnier over to cover. Allow to soak for ½ hour or longer.

Preheat the oven to 450 degrees.

TO PREPARE THE CUSTARD CUPS

Grease six 6-ounce custard cups with shortening. Place the cups in a baking pan and put them into the oven to preheat while you prepare the batter.

TO PREPARE THE BATTER

In a medium size mixing bowl, combine the eggs, milk and cooking oil. Add the flour and the salt and beat until smooth.

TO BAKE

Carefully remove the hot baking pan from the oven and fill the hot custard cups ½ full with batter. Bake in the fully preheated 450 degree oven for 20 minutes. Reduce the oven temperature to 350 degrees and bake another 15 to 20 minutes or until the popovers are very firm. If the popovers brown too quickly, turn the oven off and allow them to finish baking in the oven as it cools. A few minutes before removing from the oven, prick each popover with a fork to allow steam to escape.

Serve the popovers hot from the oven with the marinated fresh fruits and dusted with powdered sugar.

KEEPSAKE SOUR CREAM COFFEE CAKE

YIELD: 8 TO 12 SERVINGS

½ CUP (I STICK) BUTTER
1 CUP SUGAR
2 EGGS
1 TEASPOON VANILLA
2 TBS. FRESH LEMON JUICE
2 CUPS ALL-PURPOSE FLOUR
1 TEASPOON BAKING POWDER
1 TEASPOON BAKING SODA
1 CUP SOUR CREAM

BRAN AND PECAN TOPPING

¾ CUP BROWN SUGAR
1 TABLESPOON FLOUR
1 TEASPOON CINNAMON
2 TABLESPOONS BUTTER
1 CUP CHOPPED PECANS

COFFEE CAKE LADY

Her coffee cake had no rivalry
Across the years, but is secure as when
She handed its light, fragrant loaf to me
With, "Take this to your Mother."
Now and then a modern version
Of her art has graced
The table and some one praised it , without doubt, -
But something sweet and haunting in the taste
Of the coffee cake she baked us is left out.

Perhaps it sprang from skill that she acquired
In the old country when she was far younger,
It may have been that she and elves conspired,
It could have been that to my childhood hunger
It seemed so satisfying that a bit
Of glory has attached itself to it!

- Elaine V. Emans

Preheat the oven to 350 degrees. Butter a 9 inch tube pan, or a 9 inch round or square pan.

TO PREPARE THE BATTER

Cream together the butter and sugar. Add the eggs, one at a time, scraping the bowl after each addition. Blend in the vanilla and the lemon juice.

Sift together the flour, baking powder and soda. Add this to the creamed mixture blending just until smooth. Gently mix in the sour cream, being careful not to over-mix. Spread this mixture into the prepared pan.

TO PREPARE THE TOPPING

Toss together the brown sugar, flour and cinnamon. Cut in the butter, then add the pecans and sprinkle the topping onto the batter.

TO BAKE

Bake in the preheated oven for 35 to 45 minutes or until the coffee cake springs back when lightly touched in the center.

LACEY APPLE STRUDEL

YIELD: 20 SERVINGS

PASTRY DOUGH

1 CUP (2 STICKS) COLD BUTTER

2 CUPS ALL-PURPOSE FLOUR

1 CUP SOUR CREAM

CINNAMON SUGAR MIXTURE

¼ TEASPOON CINNAMON

3 TABLESPOONS SUGAR

ON OPENING A SACK OF FLOUR

That a miller's a magician,
Flour is proof enough:
From hardest golden kernels
He turns out such stuff
As looks and feels as it might be
Ground-up thistle fluff.

- Ethel Romig Fuller

PASTRY FILLING

> 4 CUPS FINELY DICED TART GREEN APPLES
>
> 2 TABLESPOONS FRESH LEMON JUICE
>
> ¾ CUP FINE DRY BREAD CRUMBS
>
> ¼ CUP BROWN SUGAR
>
> ¼ CUP WHITE SUGAR
>
> 2 TEASPOONS CINNAMON
>
> 2 TEASPOONS VANILLA
>
> ¾ CUP CURRANTS OR RAISINS
>
> ½ CUP FINELY CHOPPED WALNUTS

EGG WASH

> 1 EGG
>
> 2 TABLESPOONS COLD WATER
>
> POWDERED SUGAR FOR DUSTING

TO PREPARE THE PASTRY

Put the flour into the bowl of an electric mixer. Cut the butter into small pieces and add it to the flour. On low speed, mix the two together until it resembles coarse meal. Add the sour cream and mix only until the dough forms a ball. On a lightly floured board, knead briefly. Wrap the dough in plastic and chill thoroughly if needed.

On a lightly floured surface roll the pastry into a very thin rectangle, 19 inches by 22 inches. Trim the pastry into an even rectangle, saving the scraps to decorate the top. Cut the dough in half the long way. Mix the cinnamon with the sugar and sprinkle it evenly over the two dough sections.

TO PREPARE THE FILLING, ASSEMBLE AND BAKE

Mix all the filling ingredients together in the order given. Divide the filling between the two sections and spread an even strip down the middle. Roll the pastry and place it seam side down onto a sheet pan lined with parchment paper or an ungreased baking sheet. Preheat the oven to 400 degrees.

Thoroughly beat together the egg and cold water. Cut the scraps into decorative shapes and place them in a pretty pattern on top of the pastry, brushing them with egg wash to make them stick. Lightly brush the entire pastry again, evenly, so that they will brown uniformly.

Bake in the fully preheated oven for 20 to 25 minutes, or until lightly golden and the filling starts to bubble. Cool slightly, then dust with powdered sugar and cut into diagonal pieces.

MILLER'S ENGLISH BRAN MUFFINS

FIELD: EIGHT 4 INCH MUFFINS

GIVE US THIS DAY OUR DAILY BREAD

1 TABLESPOON YEAST
½ CUP WARM WATER
1 TABLESPOON HONEY
½ CUP HOT WATER
½ CUP COLD MILK
½ CUP BRAN
1½ CUPS WHOLE WHEAT FLOUR
1 TEASPOON SALT
½ TEASPOON BAKING SODA
1½ CUPS ALL PURPOSE FLOUR
YELLOW CORN MEAL FOR DUSTING

Back of the dough is the shining flour,
And back of the flour is the mill,
And back of the mill are the wind and shower,
And the sun, and the Father's will.

- Maltbie Babcock

TOPPINGS

RICOTTA CHEESE
MARMALADE
TOASTED SUNFLOWER SEEDS
CINNAMON

TO PREPARE THE MUFFINS

Sprinkle the yeast over the ½ cup warm water, stir in the honey and let this mixture rise until foamy.

In a large mixing bowl, stir together the ½ cup hot tap water with the cold milk, adjusting the temperature if needed, so the mixture feels warm to the touch, but not hot. Stir in the foamy yeast mixture, bran, and whole wheat flour and continue beating in a circular, clockwise motion until the ingredients are well incorporated. Continue beating 200 strokes.

Cover this "sponge" with a clean tea towel and let rest until the mixture starts to rise, then beat in the salt, baking soda, and enough of the white flour to make a kneadable dough. Turn out onto a floured board and knead well, about 10 minutes. Place the dough into a lightly oiled bowl, turning once to oil the top. Cover and let rise until doubled.

Punch down the dough and roll it out to a ½ inch thickness. Cut the dough into circles with a four-inch English muffin or biscuit cutter and transfer the rounds to a surface that has been generously sprinkled with corn meal. Cover the rounds with a tea towel and let rise until almost doubled.

TO COOK

Wipe the insides of a heavy skillet with oil, removing any excess. Dust with the cornmeal and heat it over medium heat, carefully adjusting the heat so the cornmeal doesn't burn. Carefully lift the rounds with a flat turner to the skillet, and toast both sides until golden. Add more cornmeal to the pan if necessary to keep the muffins from sticking. Remove and let cool on a rack, then split the muffins open with a fork and toast. To serve, spread with ricotta and marmalade and sprinkle with toasted sunflower seeds and cinnamon, or, spread with butter, honey or with jam.

BIG HEARTED CINNAMON ROLLS

YIELD: 1 DOZEN

1 CUP MILK
⅔ CUP (1½ STICKS) BUTTER
⅔ CUP SUGAR
1½ TEASPOONS SALT
2 EGGS, BEATEN
2 TABLESPOONS YEAST
1 CUP WARM WATER
7 CUPS WHITE, ALL PURPOSE FLOUR

FILLING

1 CUP (2 STICKS) BUTTER
1 CUP BROWN SUGAR
1 TABLESPOON CINNAMON
1½ TEASPOONS VANILLA
1 CUP RAISINS
¾ CUP CHOPPED WALNUTS

GLAZE

1 BOX POWDERED SUGAR
½ CUP ORANGE JUICE

THOSE LUSCIOUS LOAVES

What fragrant viands Mom could make,
Cinnamon rolls, cinnamon cake,
Devil's food and angels food,
And nothing hit-or-miss or crude,
But everything quite heavenly fit,
Beautiful and exquisite.

And when she tilted back the bin,
Dipping her sifter out and in,
Ah, what a fluffy, snow-white tower
Rose up before her in that flour.
And what a promise blossomed there
To make a youngster's childhood fair.

On cookie day who could refrain
From lingering, in sun or rain,
Around the kitchen counter, strewn
With cutters, mixing bowl, and spoon -
And who could ever wear a frown
Munching hot cookies, white or brown.

But Mother, smiling, often said
Her pride and joy was making bread;
Hence mixing, kneading, and what not,
Keeping the baking oven hot,
Found her divinely flushed and cheered
When all those luscious loaves appeared.

- Edwin T. Reed

TO PREPARE THE DOUGH

In a small saucepan, scald the milk by heating it gently until tiny bubbles appear around the outside edges. Cut the butter into small pieces and place them into a large bowl, along with the sugar and salt. Pour in the hot milk and stir to dissolve the butter. When the hot mixture has cooled, beat in the eggs.

In a small bowl, sprinkle the yeast over the warm water and let set until foamy, then add it to the cooled milk mixture. Stir in 1 cup at a time, enough of the white flour to make a kneadable dough. Turn the dough out onto a lightly floured board and knead, flouring the board from time to time to keep the dough from sticking, until smooth and elastic. Place the dough into a lightly oiled bowl, turning it once to oil the top. Cover the bowl with a clean tea towel and let rise until doubled.

TO PREPARE THE FILLING

Prepare the filling while the dough is rising so that it has time to cool. In a small saucepan over low heat, melt together the butter and brown sugar. Stir in the cinnamon, vanilla, raisins and walnuts. Let cool.

TO ASSEMBLE, BAKE AND GLAZE

When the dough has doubled in bulk, punch it down and briefly knead out any air bubbles. Roll the dough into a 12 inch by 14 inch rectangle. Spread the cooled filling onto the dough, leaving a clean 1 inch rim along the long side. Roll the dough up tightly. Pinch the clean seam gently to seal. Slice the dough with a sharp knife into 12 equal portions and place, cut-side down, on a half-sheet pan lined with parchment paper, or lightly grease a baking sheet. Cover with a clean tea towel and let rise until almost doubled. While it is rising, preheat the oven to 350 degrees. Bake the cinnamon rolls for 20 to 30 minutes, or until golden. Cool to warm before glazing. To prepare the glaze, beat together the powdered sugar and the orange juice until completely smooth. With a fork or your fingers, drizzle the glaze over the warm, but not too hot, rolls.

PECAN STICKY BUNS

YIELD 24 BUNS

PAN FILLING

½ CUP BUTTER
½ CUP GRANULATED SUGAR
1 TEASPOON CINNAMON
⅔ CUP BROWN SUGAR
⅓ CUP HONEY
1 CUP CHOPPED PECANS
1 TABLESPOON VANILLA

DOUGH FILLING

¼ CUP BUTTER
⅓ CUP GRANULATED SUGAR
½ TEASPOON CINNAMON

BAKING DAY

What shall I bake for three little-girls
With impish smiles and cherubic curls
And twinkly eyes and twinkly feet,
Cinnamon buns are the perfect treat!

Fat little buns all sugar and spice
And honey and currants, everything nice -
For that's what little-girls. everyone knows,
Have always been made of from tops to toes.

- Ethel Jacobson

TO PREPARE THE DOUGH

Prepare one recipe of CINNAMON ROLL DOUGH (page 93) and let it rise until almost doubled.

TO PREPARE THE PAN FILLING

 While the dough is rising, prepare the pan filling by gently melting together the pan filling ingredients in the order given. Divide the pan filling evenly into the bottoms of 2 muffin pans, (24 cups), and let cool.

TO PREPARE THE DOUGH FILLING

After the dough has doubled in bulk, knead briefly to remove any air bubbles. Roll the dough into a rectangle. Gently melt the ¼ cup of butter and brush it on the rolled out dough.

Mix together the sugar and cinnamon and sprinkle it evenly on the dough, leaving a 1 inch rim the length of the dough. Roll the dough up tightly. Slice the dough with a sharp knife into 24 even pieces. Place the pieces, cut side down into the prepared muffin pans, cover with a clean tea towel and let rise until almost doubled. While the buns are rising, preheat the oven to 350 degrees.

TO BAKE

Bake the rolls in the fully preheated oven for 18 to 20 minutes, or until golden. Cool slightly before inverting the pans on cooling racks.

MOMENT RECAPTURED

An old man rocks there in the sun;
The chairs slow creaking takes him back:
He stands inside his father's mill
And listens to the great wheel clack.

The sun streams through the window pane
And shows the dust motes all a-dance.
Noise and motion? Yes, but now
It seems to him like real romance.

– Eloise Wade Hackett

CHAPTER TWO

SCRUMPTIOUS MUFFINS

DEDICATED TO THE STAFFORD COUNTY FLOUR MILLS

EST. 1905

STAFFORD COUNTY FLOUR MILLS

Today, two-thirds of the Stafford County Flour Mill's total production is sent to West Virginia, Virginia, Kentucky, Tennessee, Pennsylvania, Ohio, and North Carolina, where great biscuit-making is a daily art.

While many of the small mills that once dotted the Kansas plains have vanished, Stafford County operates around the clock most days to keep up with the demand for its flour. Hudson Cream is the pride of the Stafford County Flour Mill Company in the central Kansas town of Hudson, the only independently owned mill remaining in the Wheat State.

The gleaming elevators of the Stafford County Flour Mills Company tower above the golden wheat fields on the Kansas prairie. The silos are the same color as the mill's white, rich flour.

Gustav Krug, who immigrated to Stafford County in 1882 from Saxony, Germany, and his brother-in-law, Otto Sonderegger, started the Hudson Milling Company in 1905.

The original mill was a wooden structure that produced 75 barrels, or 150 hundredweigh (cwt), of flour daily. Krug didn't have the benefit of a conveniently located stream to run a mill wheel, so he powered it with steam. The wheat was purchased locally and hauled in by the railroad and horse-drawn wagons. The flour was sold locally, mostly in 100-pound cotton sacks.

The Hudson Flour Milling Company became the Stafford County Flour Mill Company in 1909, when Krug sold stock to local investors. A rash of fires plagued the town of Hudson in 1913, and the mill was one of the victims. Locals thought Krug, then nearly 70 years old, would close the mill. Instead, he found investors and in 1914, opened a modern concrete mill capable of producing 600 cwts. of flour daily.

In the years that followed, the mill experienced steady growth by selling flour to home bakers and expanded its market to five other states.

In 1964, Buhler-Miag installed modern automation, and the mills production expanded to 1,000 cwt. per day. Wheat storage was gradually expanded to its current on-site capacity of 1 million bushels and another 800,000 in Macksville, a neighboring town.

The year 1984 saw the installation of automated flour packaging equipment in a new structure. Demand kept growing, and more structures were added in 1992 to house the cleaning and tempering equipment. New milling equipment was installed, and the mill now produces 2,400 cwts daily, with the potential to produce 5,000 cwt. The mill operates around the clock.

RICHES OF MEMORY

I have been given a wealth so rare
No thief could ever guess or see.
I hoard it against the day of need -
The riches of memory.
Sunset beyond a corn-shocked field,
A distant church's burnished spire,
A sumac bush flaming beside
An elm tree's yellow fire;
A plume of smoke, a lighted pane,
Evening sounds, stars overhead,
A kitchen bright with homey cheer
And sweet with the smell of new baked bread.

- Maude Greene Princehouse

PROPER BAKING PROCEDURES FOR MUFFINS

PREHEATING THE OVEN

Start preheating the oven in plenty of time so that it reaches the correct temperature before the muffins go into the oven. The instant high heat is essential to develop the desired crown, the signature of a good muffin. Be sure your oven rack is in the center position.

PREPARING THE PANS

Most muffins seem to turn out best and have the nicest crown when baking cup liners are used to line the muffin cups. If you are making heavier muffins, such as corn, grease the cups lightly with shortening. Be sure to also lightly grease the rims around the edges of each cup so that the muffin tops don't stick.

Prepare the pans before you mix the muffin batter. Once the batter has been mixed it should not be allowed to sit, because the leavening agent becomes activated and loses its strength.

MIXING THE MUFFIN DOUGH

Be sure not to over-mix the batter. Pour the wet ingredients into the dry and mix only enough to moisten. This keeps the muffins tender. Scoop the batter into the prepared pans and put them into the preheated oven as quickly as possible.

DIVIDING THE BATTER

Using a large ice cream scoop to divide the batter evenly also gives the muffins a nice rounded appearance. Divide the batter equally between the cups so all the muffins will be the same size and bake evenly. Be sure to fill the muffin cups ⅔ full.

CHECKING FOR DONENESS

The muffins have finished baking when the center is firm when lightly touched, or when a tester inserted in the center comes out clean.

COOLING AND STORING

Cool slightly before removing the muffins from the cups. If necessary, run a knife around the top edge to loosen them. Serve warm. Cool completely before storing. Any leftovers may be wrapped in foil to be gently reheated before serving at another time.

MUFFINS - For decades the tintinnabulating muffin man was a familiar character in every British urban street. The welcome sound of his jingling bell was the signal for mother to make urgent progress to the front door to purchase some of his delicious wares for the family tea.

The muffin! Toasted and eaten piping hot with rivulets of golden butter cascading through its many pours: the warm aroma of sunbathed wheat fields delighting the nostrils and the soft sinking of teeth into succulent flesh symbolic of the good things that from the earth do come.

- The Northwestern Miller

SPICY PEAR MUFFINS

MUFFIN BATTER

YIELD: 18 MUFFINS

4 LARGE PEARS PEELED, CORED AND DICED
1 CUP SUGAR
½ CUP VEGETABLE OIL
2 LARGE EGGS, BEATEN TO BLEND
2 TEASPOONS VANILLA EXTRACT
1 CUP RAISINS
1 CUP CHOPPED WALNUTS
2 CUPS ALL-PURPOSE FLOUR
2 TEASPOONS BAKING SODA
2 TEASPOONS GROUND CINNAMON
1 TEASPOON GROUND NUTMEG
1 TEASPOON SALT

Preheat the oven to 325 degrees.

TO PREPARE THE MUFFIN PANS

Line 18 muffin cups with paper, or grease them generously.

TO PREPARE THE MUFFIN BATTER

Mix the diced pears and sugar in a medium-size bowl. In a large bowl whisk together the oil, eggs and vanilla.

Sift together the flour, baking soda, cinnamon, nutmeg and salt.

Stir the pear mixture into the egg mixture. Mix in the raisins and walnuts.

Pour the dry ingredients into the wet and mix only enough to moisten. Divide the batter between the prepared muffin cups.

TO BAKE

Bake the muffins in the preheated oven until the center is light to the touch, or a tester inserted in the center comes out clean, about 30 minutes.

SPICE MADE HISTORY

History writes words like these:
Ceylon, Sumatra, Celebes!
Nutmeg, ginger, cinnamon!...
Rides many a ghostly galleon
Manned by crews who died to bring
Aromatics, that a king,
Apt to humor, might have sup
If red wine, mulled within the cup...
That priests might burn before their Lord
His need of incense, by the sword
Men lived and died. Their blood was price
Of precious bark and berry. Spice
Made history dark with words like these:
Ceylon, Sumatra, Celebes!

– Phyllis B. Morden

ZESTY BLUEBERRY MUFFINS

MUFFIN BATTER

YIELD: 20 MUFFINS

4 CUPS UNBLEACHED, ALL-PURPOSE FLOUR
1 TABLESPOON DOUBLE-ACTING BAKING POWDER
1 TEASPOON CINNAMON
1 TEASPOON SALT
1½ CUPS SUGAR
½ CUP POWDERED MILK
8 OUNCES (2 STICKS) BUTTER
3 EGGS
1½ CUPS WATER
2 TEASPOONS VANILLA
JUICE AND ZEST OF 1 LEMON
4 CUPS BLUEBERRIES
POWDERED SUGAR FOR DUSTING

IT BEATS 'EM ALL

I like the scent of roses
Fresh with the morning dew;
Brown, burning leaves some noses
Find quite appealing, too.

But the scent which is breath-taking,
To get enraptured o'er
Is that of muffin's baking,
When one opens the oven door!
O that crispy, pungent savor
Which makes one sniff with joy!
That appetizing flavor
Which appeals to girl and boy!

You may have your aromatic
Perfumes which rare flowers shed;
But for me the smell ecstatic
Is hot-crusted muffin bread!

- Clarence Mansfield Lindsey

Preheat the oven to 400 degrees. Line 20 muffin cups with paper or grease with shortening.

Sift together the flour, baking powder, cinnamon, and salt.

In the bowl of an electric mixer mix together the sugar and powdered milk. Add the butter and beat until light. Add the eggs, one at a time, scraping the bowl after each addition. Mix the water with the vanilla, lemon juice and zest and slowly mix it in. Add the flour mixture and mix just until creamy. Fold in the blueberries.

Scoop into the prepared muffin cups. Bake in the fully preheated oven for 20 to 25 minutes or until firm to the touch and lightly golden. Cool some before removing from the pans.

Dust with powdered sugar if desired.

TENDER BERRY MUFFINS

MUFFIN BATTER

YIELD: 12 MUFFINS

2 CUPS ALL-PURPOSE FLOUR
2 TEASPOONS BAKING POWDER
½ TEASPOON SALT
1 CUP SUGAR
½ TEASPOON CINNAMON
½ CUP (1 STICK) BUTTER, MELTED
1 CUP MILK
1 EGG
1 TEASPOON VANILLA
ZEST OF ONE LEMON
2 CUPS FRESH OR FROZEN BLACKBERRIES
POWDERED SUGAR FOR DUSTING (OPTIONAL)

Preheat the oven to 385 degrees.

TO PREPARE THE PANS.

Line one 12 cup muffin pan with paper or foil liners.

TO PREPARE THE BATTER

In a large bowl, mix together the flour, baking powder, salt, sugar and cinnamon. In another bowl, whisk together the melted butter, milk, egg, vanilla and the lemon zest. Pour the wet ingredients into the dry and mix only enough to moisten. Fold in the fresh or frozen berries, being careful not to over-mix. With an ice cream scoop, divide the batter evenly between the papered muffin pans.

TO BAKE

Bake the muffins in the fully preheated 385 degree oven approximately 15 to 20 minutes or until done. To check for doneness, the muffin crown should have a nice golden color and the muffins should spring back when lightly touched on the top. Cool slightly before removing from the pans.

DUSTING WITH POWDERED SUGAR

If desired, dust with powdered sugar when cool.

CONCERNING MILADY'S SPRING HAT

I've seen them with berries,
I've see them with cherries,
With peaches and apricots, too
I've see them with grapes
Of different shapes
In a green or a violet hue.

Why shouldn't a bonnet
Have heads of flax on it,
Or millet or barley or rye?
And a little gold cluster
Of wheat would add luster
To any chapeau passing by.

An embellishing biscuit?
Milady might risk it,
Or a muffin or strawberry tart.
For a hat pastry-scented
Would have unprecedented
Appeal to the masculine heart!

- Grace V. Watkins

HARVEST MOON PUMPKIN MUFFINS

MUFFIN BATTER

YIELD: 12 MUFFINS

1 CUP GOLDEN RAISINS
½ CUP HOT WATER
1¾ CUPS ALL-PURPOSE FLOUR
1½ TEASPOONS BAKING POWDER
1¼ CUPS SUGAR
1 TEASPOON SALT
½ TEASPOON BAKING SODA
½ TEASPOON GROUND CLOVES
¾ TEASPOON CINNAMON
1 CUP CANNED PUMPKIN
½ CUP PLUS 2 TABLESPOONS VEGETABLE OIL
2 EGGS
½ CUP CHOPPED WALNUTS

HARVEST EVE

Wheat ripples like a tawny hide
Upon the dark-fleshed earth,
feeling the subtly prickling tide
Of wind's disturbing mirth:

Feeling a portent of adieu
To summer growth and grain:
To nights of starry rendezvous:
To whisperings of rain.

The stubble's sharp bewildered spell
Chills through the waiting leaves,
Recalling other wheat that fell
In harvest-ravished sheaves.

- Maud E. Uschold

Preheat the oven to 400 degrees

TO PREPARE THE MUFFIN PANS

Line one 12 cup muffin pan with paper liners.

TO PREPARE THE BATTER

Soak the raisins in the hot water for 10 minutes or until plump.

In a large bowl, sift together the flour, baking powder, sugar, salt, baking soda, ground cloves and cinnamon. In another large bowl, beat together the pumpkin, oil, eggs and chopped nuts. Drain the raisins and add them to the mixture.

Add the wet ingredients to the dry and mix only enough to moisten.

With an ice cream scoop divide the batter evenly between the 12 papered cups.

TO BAKE

Bake the muffins in the fully preheated oven for 15 to 20 minutes or until the centers are firm to the touch.

SUMPTUOUS BRAN MUFFINS

MUFFIN BATTER

YIELD: 12 MUFFINS

1 CUP BRAN
1 CUP BUTTERMILK
⅓ CUP (⅔ STICK) BUTTER
½ CUP BROWN SUGAR
¼ CUP MOLASSES
1 EGG
1 CUP ALL-PURPOSE FLOUR
1 TEASPOON CINNAMON
1 TEASPOON BAKING POWDER
½ TEASPOON BAKING SODA
½ TEASPOON SALT
⅔ CUP RAISINS

Preheat the oven to 400 degrees.

BAKER WOMAN

Familiar, bone deep
As telling her beads,
There's a rhythm to bread
As the old woman kneads.
The dough she patted,
The bowls are scraped.
What a lifetime of loaves
Her hands have shaped.
Hands like brown birds,
But deft and strong
On the worn, floured board
They strum out their song.
While a cat on the doorsill
Suns and purrs,
Kneading with paws
As rhythmic as hers.

- Ethel Jacobson

TO PREPARE THE MUFFIN PANS

Line one 12 cup muffin pan with foil or paper liners.

TO PREPARE THE BATTER

In a small bowl, mix the bran and buttermilk together and allow this mixture to sit for ten minutes.

In a large mixing bowl, cream together the butter and the brown sugar. Add the molasses and the egg, scraping the bowl after each addition.

Sift together the flour, cinnamon, baking powder, baking soda, and salt.

Pour the bran mixture into the dry ingredients and stir just until moistened. Add this mixture to the creamed sugar mixture, along with the raisins and once again, stir only enough to blend.

With an ice cream scoop, divide the batter between the 12 lined muffin cups.

TO BAKE

Bake the muffins in the fully preheated oven for 20 to 25 minutes, or until the centers are firm to the touch.

CRANBERRY ORANGE MUFFINS

MUFFIN BATTER

YIELD: 8 LARGE OR 12 SMALL MUFFINS

1 CUP CHOPPED, FRESH CRANBERRIES
⅓ CUP SUGAR
2 CUPS ALL-PURPOSE FLOUR
½ CUP BROWN SUGAR
½ CUP WHEAT GERM
½ TEASPOON SALT
½ TEASPOON BAKING SODA
2 TEASPOON BAKING POWDER
⅓ CUP OIL
¾ CUP ORANGE JUICE
1 EGG, LIGHTLY BEATEN
2 TEASPOONS ORANGE ZEST
1 TEASPOON VANILLA

THE HEART OF THE HOME

This is the heart of home, this sunny room,
With painted cupboards and a spotless floor,
With shining pans, a yellow-handled broom,
A pot of geraniums before
An open window; an aroma spun
Of garden breezes, soap, of simmering broth;
Of mingled ginger, cloves and cinnamon
From cup cakes turned out warm upon a cloth.

A sunny room, a cheery kettle song,
A woman, love, a hearthfire's radiance –
From these a man goes forth to labor, strong;
A child to play upon tiptoes a-dance.
Beneath a cottage roof, a palace dome,
A kitchen is the heart of any home.

- Ethel Romig Fuller

TO PREPARE THE MUFFIN PANS

Line one 12 cup muffin pan with paper liners.

TO PREPARE THE BATTER

In a large bowl, mix together the cranberries and the sugar and let them set for a few minutes to develop the juices.

In another bowl, mix together the flour, brown sugar, wheat germ, salt, baking soda and baking powder.

To the cranberry-sugar mixture add the oil, orange juice, egg, grated orange zest and vanilla and stir to mix well.

Add the wet ingredients to the dry and mix only enough to moisten. With an ice cream scoop, divide the batter evenly between the prepared muffin cups.

TO BAKE

Bake in the fully preheated oven for 15 to 20 minutes, depending on the size of your muffin cups. The centers should be firm to the touch.

MORNING GLORY MUFFINS

MUFFIN BATTER

YIELD: 8 SMALL OR 12 TINY MUFFINS

½ CUP RAISINS
HOT WATER TO COVER
2 CUPS FLOUR
1 CUP SUGAR
2 TEASPOONS BAKING SODA
2 TEASPOONS CINNAMON
½ TEASPOON SALT
2 CUPS GRATED, PEELED CARROTS
1 LARGE TART GREEN APPLE, CORED AND GRATED
½ CUP SLICED ALMONDS
½ CUP SWEETENED, SHREDDED COCONUT
3 EGGS
⅔ CUP OIL
2 TEASPOONS VANILLA

Preheat the oven to 375 degrees.

TO PREPARE THE MUFFIN PANS

Generously grease muffin tins or line them with paper baking cups.

TO PREPEARE THE MUFFIN BATTER

In a small bowl, pour very hot water over the raisins to cover and let them to soak for 30 minutes, thoroughly drain the raisins and allow them to cool.

In a large bowl, mix together the flour, sugar, baking soda, cinnamon and salt. Stir in the grated carrots, apple, almonds, coconut and raisins.

Beat the eggs with the oil and vanilla to blend. Stir the egg mixture into the flour mixture just until incorporated. Scoop the batter into the prepared muffin cups, filling the cups until almost full.

TO BAKE

Bake in the fully preheated oven approximately 20 minutes, or just until golden brown and firm to the touch. Cool for 5 minutes before removing from the pans. Serve warm or at room temperature.

NEIGHBORS

This has become the outward sign
I am her neighbor and she is mine:
It's the custom, now, for me to take
Her golden muffins when I bake,
And likely as not, when she makes plum
Preserves or jell she brings me some.
But dearer than our gifts and speech
Is love within us, each for each.

- Elaine V. Emans

OLD MILLS

Whenever a miller dammed a lively stream
The wilderness responded. Drawn to his wheel–
Filings to magnet–settlers came by team
Or horseback, bringing their grain for flour and meal.
Soon by the pond a busy village grew
As carpenter and blacksmith settled down.
A tavern throve, a church. a store or two,
For a mill was often father to a town.

Mighty are mills now rumbling night and day
To rid our world of hunger's undertones,
Yet memory treasures well the leisured way
Of little mills with slow-revolving stones
Timed to their water-wheels. Who has not heard
The drip from paddles turned by mill-race power
Has missed a soft interpretive word –
Romance....romance... in every sack of flour.

- Eloise Wade Hackett

CHAPTER THREE

TASTY TEA BREADS

DEDICATED TO THE WALL-ROGALSKY MILLING COMPANY

EST. 1906

THE WALL-ROGALSKY MILLING COMPANY

The Wall-Rogalsky Milling Company, established in 1906, has been in the flour milling business in McPherson, Kansas for 93 years.

The Company is part of the great heritage which Kansas agriculture and industry gained from the Mennonite migrations of the 1870's. John J. Wall was brought to this country in 1874 by his parents, who were wheat growers. Some of them were millers, and together they pioneered hard winter wheat production in Kansas.

J.J. Wall became a farmer, carpenter, and thresher. In 1885, when the Welk and Weins gristmill in the Buhler community fell into financial straits, Mr. Wall, at the age of 23, was named receiver. Mr. Wall hired a young miller, Herman Rogalsky, who had been operating a water mill in Marion, Kansas.

Together they operated the Welk and Weins mill for some years with financial success. They later bought the mill from the bankruptcy court and formed The Wall-Rogalsky Milling Company.

By 1905, Mr. Wall saw a need for better access to the railroads and chose McPherson as the site for a new mill. Construction on the new mill began in 1905 and operations began in 1906, with John J. Wall as business manager and Herman Rogalsky as head miller. The new mill, considered the finest in the state, required several rail car loads of heavy timber. The mill was built with the most up-to-date machinery and employed the roller process to do the grinding. Equipped with 9 sets of 36" wheat rolls and one corn roll, power was furnished by a two hundred horsepower Allis-Chalmers steam engine. The new mill had a milling capacity of 800 cwts. per day and wheat storage for about 370,000 bushels. In 1995, the mill completed an expansion project and now has a capacity of 4,600 cwts. per day.

The Wall-Rogalsky Milling Company is one of the oldest industries in the City of McPherson. John J. Wall, (1862-1916), was a sound businessman and entrepreneur with a penchant for the future. He retained a pulse of what was to come, which carried over through him to future generations. His oldest son, Ernest A. Wall, served as president of the company from 1925 to 1967 when John B. Wall, his second son, was named president. In 1983, J. Brent Wall, son of John B. Wall, was elected president. Ernest Wall's grandson, Eric A. Wall, is vice president of sales. From the time of Mr. Wall's death, in 1916, C. A. Heibert served as president until 1925. Other officers and management today are H. Wayne Ford, vice president; C.B. Spillman, Secretary-treasurer; and Max Streit, plant manager.

The mill produces flour for bakeries, consumer flour for home use, and flour for institutional use. Sales extend through the central states to the eastern seaboard, from the Canadian border to the Texas gulf. Current mill brands are W-R, Utility, America's Best, Kansas Sun, and Bake-Rite. The mill also produces private label flour for various customers.

At present, The Wall Rogalsky Milling Company is one of three independently owned flour mills in Kansas. The Wall family has always had the philosophy to be open to change, adapt to customer needs, update operations and plan and build for the future. The Wall Rogalsky Milling Company will celebrate their Centennial in the year 2006.

NEW YEAR'S EVE

Only an hour, and the white new year
Will come, quite as prairie snow,
And you and I across the table here
Beside the fire will feel the slow
Pulse of the universe, the mystic rhyme
Of space, the soundless rhapsody of time.

And then before the rite of breaking bread,
Our lips will move in low sweet prayer
That everywhere on land and sea,
all peoples may be fed.

– Grace V. Watkins

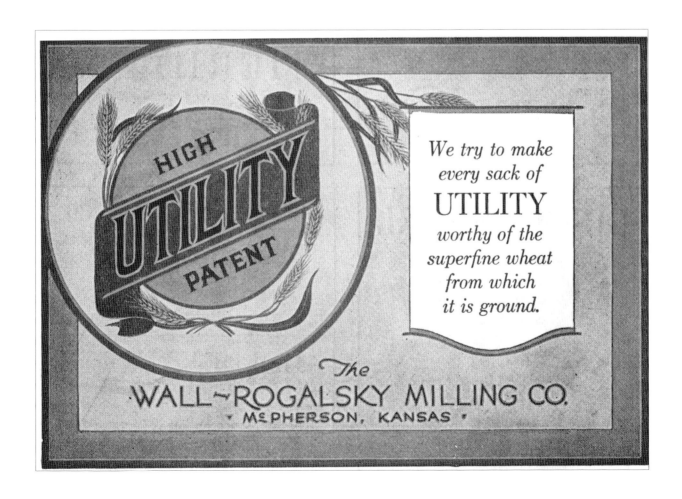

PROPER BAKING PROCEDURES FOR TEA BREADS

PREHEATING THE OVEN

Start preheating the oven in plenty of time so that it reaches the correct temperature before you put the loaves into the oven. The leavening agents used need the instant high heat in order for the breads to rise properly. Always be sure your oven rack is in the center position.

PREPARING THE PANS

Lightly grease the pans with shortening, being sure to grease the corners. Oil makes the loaves stick, and butter, because of it's low burning point, will cause them to burn.

MIXING THE TEA BREAD BATTER

To insure lightness, mix tea bread or quick bread batter just enough for the wet ingredients to moisten the dry. Over-mixing will allow the gases to escape, and it also develops the gluten, which will cause the quick breads to be heavy.

FILLING THE PANS

Be sure to fill whatever pans you use only ¾'s full. This allows the loaves room to rise so they will have a full, rounded appearance.

SCORING

In the oven, when quick and tea breads bake, the outside of the loaves form a crust. Professional bakers "score" their loaves to get maximum crowning and to make sure the tops of the loaves don't split. To do this, you simply coat a scraper, spatula or large knife by dipping it in oil, then push it once, lengthwise, through the center of the batter. The oil released in the middle of the loaf allows the insides to rise, before the top is sealed, creating a more attractive top. If you are adding nuts to the top, this is done after the loaf has been scored.

CHECKING FOR DONENESS

The loaves have finished baking when the center top is firm to the touch.

COOLING AND STORING

The loaves will be tender when they first come out of the oven. Allow them to cool slightly before removing them from the pans. Gently run a knife around the outside edge, then turn them out onto a cooling rack. Place them right-side-up and allow them to cool some before slicing. Any leftover tea bread or quick bread should be wrapped after it has cooled completely.

FOUR P.M.

While the world beyond the windows—
The rolling wheat fields; clover meadows—
Is drifted high with wind-blown snow,
In the kitchen is a glow
Of fire-light through a cook stove door
Stippled on the clean-scrubbed floor.
A coppery tea kettle hums;
On the sill, geraniums,
Scarlet, rosy-pink and white,
Catch the last faint rays of light.
The canary softly cheeps:
On a mat, a kitten sleeps;
Without, there is a windy din—
A sense of utter peace within,
And through it all, a fragrance spread
From crusty loaves of fresh-made bread.

- Ethel Romig Fuller

SWEETHEART'S APPLE TEA RING

APPLE TEA RING BATTER

- 1 CUP PEELED, CHOPPED, RAW APPLES
- 2 CUPS SUGAR
- 3 EGGS
- 1¼ CUPS SALAD OIL
- ¼ CUP FRESH ORANGE JUICE
- 1 TEASPOON VANILLA
- 3 CUPS ALL-PURPOSE FLOUR
- 1 TEASPOON BAKING SODA
- ¼ TEASPOON SALT
- 1 TEASPOON CINNAMON
- 1 CUP SHREDDED COCONUT
- 1 CUP CHOPPED PECANS

Preheat the oven to 325 degrees.

BENEDICITE

A mug of milk and a bit of bread,
And the sweet of a pear tree close by,
A picket fence and a wide, white gate,
And a slim young moon in a solemn sky.

Tap of rain on the window pane,
Bend of trees and the swish of grass
When storm gods strive and clouds draw close
Like a pack of sheep in a narrow pass.

Orchard white, when young spring nights
Press tender lips to phantom lace.
Beat of the sea in an angry wind,
And the sting of spray on my upturned face.

Stillness of snow and cold, white stars,
Glow of log when nights are long.
Shadow sweep on the smooth of your cheek
And a glimpse of soul through the veil of song.

A mug of milk and a bit of bread,
Click o' the gate that the evening brings;
A clean white quilt on a poster bed –
Oh, God, my thanks for simple things.

- Harvey E. Yantis

TO PREPARE THE PAN

Lightly grease a 10 inch tub pan with shortening.

TO PREPARE THE BATTER

Peal, core and chop the apples to make one cup and set aside. In a large mixing bowl, beat together the sugar, eggs, salad oil, orange juice and vanilla.

Sift together the flour, baking soda, salt and cinnamon and fold them into the wet mixture, just enough to blend. Add the chopped apple, coconut and chopped pecans and carefully fold them in.

TO BAKE

Carefully pour into the prepared pan and bake in the fully preheated oven for 50-60 minutes or until the tea bread is slightly firm to the touch.

LEMONY BLUEBERRY BREAD

TEA BREAD BATTER

YIELD: ONE MEDIUM OR TWO SMALL LOAVES

2 CUPS ALL-PURPOSE FLOUR
1 TEASPOON BAKING POWDER
FINELY GRATED RIND OF 1 LEMON
FINELY GRATED RIND OF 1 ORANGE
1 CUP BUTTER, ROOM TEMPERATURE
1 CUP SUGAR
4 EGGS
1 CUP FRESH OR FROZEN BLUEBERRIES

GLAZE

¼ CUP FRESH LEMON JUICE
½ CUP POWDERED SUGAR

AXIOM

A woman has since time began,
Used fragrance to attract a man,
And though a man may follow his nose
To alter-rail and ring he goes
More docilely if he is led
By scents that rise from homemade bread.

- Eloise Wade Hackett

Preheat the oven to 350 degrees. Lightly grease one large or two small loaf pans.

TO PREPARE THE BATTER

In a small bowl, sift together the flour and baking powder and set aside. Finely grate the zest of the lemon and orange onto a piece of waxed paper and set aside.

In a large bowl, beat together the butter and sugar until light. Add the eggs, one at a time, thoroughly scraping the bottom of the bowl after each addition. Add the grated lemon and orange rind, the sifted flour and baking powder mixture and mix only enough to blend. Carefully fold in the fresh or frozen blueberries.

Pour the batter into the prepared pan or pans. Score the batter by running a spatula that has been dipped in oil, lengthwise, through the center of the loaves. Bake in the fully preheated oven for 50 minutes to one hour, or until the top of the loaves feel firm to the touch.

TO PREPARE THE GLAZE

Thoroughly mix together the lemon juice and powdered sugar. When the tea bread has finished baking, remove it from the oven and allow it to cool for five minutes in the pan. Run a knife along the sides and carefully unmold it onto a cooling rack. Place a piece of waxed paper under the rack. Pour the glaze over the tea bread. Allow the loaves to cool before slicing.

MOIST BANANA BRAN BREAD

TEA BREAD BATTER

YIELD: ONE LARGE OR TWO SMALL LOAVES

1 CUP (2 STICKS) BUTTER
½ CUP WHITE SUGAR
1 CUP BROWN SUGAR
6 TO 7 RIPE BANANAS
½ CUP BRAN
4 EGGS
2¼ CUPS ALL-PURPOSE FLOUR
2 TEASPOONS BAKING SODA
1 TEASPOON SALT
1 CUP GOLDEN RAISINS
½ CUP CHOPPED PECANS

Preheat the oven to 350 degrees.

TO PREPARE THE PANS

Lightly grease one 8 inch by 4½ inch bread pan, or two small loaf pans with shortening.

TO PREPARE THE BATTER

Cream together the butter and sugars. Add the bananas, bran and the eggs.

Sift together the flour, baking soda and salt. Add the dry ingredients to the wet, mixing only enough to moisten. Fold in the raisins.

Pour the batter into the prepared pans. Score the batter by running a spatula that has been dipped in oil, lengthwise, through the center of the loaf or loaves. Sprinkle with the chopped pecans.

TO BAKE

Bake in the fully preheated oven for 45 minutes to one hour, until the edges begin to pull away from the sides of the pan and the loaves are firm when lightly touched in the center.

Cool for five minutes before removing from the pan. Remove and cool on a rack before slicing.

WHAT'S LIFE?

What's life? To love the things we see;
The hills that touch the skies;
The smiling sea: the laughing lea;
The light in a woman's eyes.
To work and love the work we do;
To play a game that's square:
To grin a bit when feeling blue;
With friends our joys to share;
To smile, though games be lost or won;
To earn our daily bread:
And when at last the day is done
To tumble into bed.

– Griffite Alexander

WHEAT IN JUNE

Upon this slope the rain falls
With benison of prayer –
The fragrance born of growing things
Is potent in the air.

This bright green spread of beauty
That is strong growing wheat
Looks forward to the sheaves of gold –
And bread we all may eat.

-Helen Maring

PINEAPPLE ORANGE TEA BREAD

131

TEA BREAD BATTER

YIELD: 1 LARGE OR 2 SMALL LOAVES

1 CAN (1 POUND 4 OUNCES) CRUSHED PINEAPPLE
2½ CUPS ALL-PURPOSE FLOUR
¾ CUP WHEAT GERM
¾ CUP SUGAR
1 TEASPOON SALT
1 TABLESPOON BAKING POWDER
½ TEASPOON BAKING SODA
⅓ CUP BUTTER
1 EGG
1 TABLESPOON FRESHLY GRATED ORANGE PEEL
1 TEASPOON VANILLA

Preheat the oven to 350 degrees.

TO PREPARE THE PANS

Lightly grease a 9 inch by 5 inch bread pan or two small loaf pans with shortening.

TO PREPARE THE BATTER

In a small pan, gently melt the butter.

In a large bowl, mix together the flour, wheat germ, sugar, salt, baking powder and baking soda.

In another bowl, mix together the melted butter, pineapple and it's juice, egg, freshly grated orange peel and vanilla.

Mix the wet and dry ingredients together only enough to moisten. Pour the batter into the prepared pans. Score the batter by running a spatula that has been dipped in oil, lengthwise, through the center of the loaf.

TO BAKE

Bake in the fully preheated oven for one hour or more, depending on the size of the pans used, or until the loaves are firm to the touch. Cool slightly before removing from the pans. Cool on a wire rack before slicing.

ENCHANTED GARDEN ZUCCHINI BREAD

TEA BREAD BATTER

YIELD: 2 LARGE LOAVES

2 CUPS PACKED, COARSELY GRATED ZUCCHINI
3 EGGS
1 CUP OIL
2 TEASPOONS VANILLA
3 CUPS ALL-PURPOSE FLOUR
1¾ CUPS SUGAR
1 TABLESPOON BAKING SODA
¼ TEASPOON BAKING POWDER
¼ TEASPOON SALT
1 TEASPOON CINNAMON
½ CUP WALNUTS OR PECANS (OPTIONAL)

WHEAT FIELDS, JULY

In all the world, no painted scene
Hung in famous gallery,
Inspired as the hill-framed green
Of summer wheat. Transcendently
A Master Artist blended all
Nuances of one color in;
Even a golden hint of Fall-
One almost hears the reaper's din,
While fore-glimpsed-so great His skill-
Is flour, when grain is harvested,
Silvery pouring from a mill
And its transformation into bread.

- Ethel Romig Fuller

Preheat the oven to 350 degrees.

TO PREPARE THE PANS

Lightly grease two 9 inch by 5 inch bread pans with shortening.

TO PREPARE THE BATTER

Wash and coarsely grate the zucchini. In a large bowl, mix together the zucchini, eggs, oil and vanilla.

Sift together the flour, sugar, baking soda, baking powder, salt and cinnamon.

Lightly mix the dry ingredients with the wet. Do not over-mix. Pour the batter into the prepared pans. Score the loaves by running a spatula that has been dipped in oil, lengthwise, through the center of the loaf. Sprinkle with the chopped walnuts.

TO BAKE

Bake in the fully preheated 350 degree oven for approximately one hour, or until a toothpick inserted in the center comes out clean, or the center feels firm to the touch. Cool slightly before removing from the pan. Unmold onto a cooling rack and cool before slicing.

SMALL BOY IN QUICK TRANSIT

From lanes of interstellar pattern,
From roads on Jupiter and Saturn,
His thoughts return in headlong flight
At speed surpassing that of light,
And kitchenward he turns his tread
At whiff of fresh-baked gingerbread!

- Grace V. Watkins

GINGERBREAD WITH SWEET CIDER SAUCE

GINGERBREAD BATTER

YIELD: 8 TO 12 SERVINGS

3 CUPS ALL-PURPOSE FLOUR
1 CUP SUGAR
1 TEASPOON BAKING SODA
½ TEASPOON SALT
1 TABLESPOON CINNAMON
1 TEASPOON CLOVES
1 TEASPOON GINGER
1 CUP OIL
3 EGGS
1 CUP BUTTERMILK
1 CUP MOLASSES

OPTIONAL SWEET CIDER SAUCE

3 CUPS FRESH, SWEET APPLE CIDER
4 TABLESPOONS CORNSTARCH
4 ALLSPICE BERRIES, BRUISED
1 PIECE CINNAMON STICK,
   2 INCHES LONG
PINCH SALT
PINCH OF FRESHLY GRATED NUTMEG

OPTIONAL GARNISHES

UNSWEETENED WHIPPED CREAM
SLIVERS OF CRYSTALLIZED GINGER

Preheat the oven to 350 degrees.

TO PREPARE THE PAN

If the gingerbread is for a fancy occasion and you want to remove it from the pan, trace a round circle, using a 10 inch or 11 inch pan, (preferably with a removable bottom), onto a piece of parchment or baking paper. Cut out the circle. Lightly grease the sides of the pan with shortening. Fit the circle into the bottom of the pan.

For large party fare, it's fun to double or triple this gingerbread recipe, and bake it in a large wedding cake pan. For a picnic or casual affair, grease the pan with shortening.

TO PREPARE THE BATTER

Sift together the flour, sugar, baking soda, salt, cinnamon, cloves and ginger. In a separate bowl, beat together the oil, eggs, buttermilk and molasses. Mix the wet ingredients with the dry only enough to moisten, being very careful not to over-mix! Pour the batter into the prepared pan.

TO BAKE

Bake in the fully preheated oven for 35 to 45 minutes or until the center feels firm to the touch. Allow to cool before stenciling or slicing.

TO PREPARE THE CIDER SAUCE

While the gingerbread is baking, pour ¼ cup of the cider into a cup, add the cornstarch and stir with a fork until smooth. Pour the remaining cider, allspice berries, cinnamon stick, salt and nutmeg in a small saucepan. Whisk in the cornstarch mixture. Cook over medium heat, stirring constantly with a whisk, until the sauce thickens and turns translucent, about three minutes.

TO SERVE

After the gingerbread has finished baking and has cooled to warm or room temperature, cut the gingerbread into serving size pieces and place them on pretty plates. Pour sweet cider sauce onto the plate. Garnish with a dollop of unsweetened whipped cream and slivered crystallized ginger.

STENCILED LACE GINGERBREAD

TO PREPARE THE STENCIL

Using a piece of paper slightly larger than the size of the pan, fold the paper in half, then in fourths. Keeping the center tip, fold one third of the paper to the center, then the other remaining third over to meet the outside edge. Cut several decorative shapes into the folded paper, the more you cut the lacier it will be. When it is unfolded, it should resemble a giant snowflake. Iron the paper to make it as flat as possible.

TO PREPARE THE PLATE

For casual fare, the gingerbread can be dusted in the pan. If you are serving the gingerbread to the ladies at an afternoon tea, you can unmold it onto a pretty serving platter, or you can make a serving board according to the directions in the cake chapter, under Proper Baking Procedures, Making A Cake Board, page 223.

TO UNMOLD THE GINGERBREAD

After the gingerbread has completely cooled, if you did not use a pan with a removable bottom, you can unmold the gingerbread by placing a plate or board slightly larger then the size of the pan over the top. Placing one hand firmly on the center of the plate and the other hand firmly in the center of the pan; carefully flip them over. Remove the pan, then peel off the parchment or baking paper. Center the serving plate or cake board onto the gingerbread, then firmly grasping the serving plate, gingerbread and top plate, flip them back over. Remove the top plate.

TO STENCIL THE GINGERBREAD

Center the prepared, ironed stencil on the cooled gingerbread. Using a sifter, gently dust the top with generous amounts of powdered sugar. Carefully remove the stencil.

SPICED PUMPKIN PECAN CAKE
WITH BUTTERMILK GLAZE

PUMPKIN CAKE BATTER

2 CUPS CHOPPED PECANS

3½ CUPS ALL-PURPOSE FLOUR

2 TEASPOONS BAKING POWDER

2 TEASPOONS BAKING SODA

1 TEASPOON SALT

2 TEASPOONS CINNAMON

½ TEASPOON NUTMEG

½ TEASPOON CLOVES

½ TEASPOON GINGER

½ TEASPOON ALLSPICE

1 CUP UNSALTED BUTTER (2 STICKS)

1¼ CUPS SUGAR

½ CUP FIRMLY PACKED BROWN SUGAR

4 LARGE EGGS, ROOM TEMPERATURE

1⅔ CUPS CANNED SOLID PACK PUMPKIN

½ CUP SOUR CREAM

¼ CUP MOLASSES

2 TABLESPOONS DARK RUM

OPTIONAL BUTTERMILK GLAZE

6 TABLESPOONS BUTTER
1 CUP SUGAR
½ TEASPOON BAKING SODA
½ CUP BUTTERMILK

Position a rack in the lower third of your oven and preheat to 350 degrees.

TO PREPARE THE PAN

Place ½ cup of the chopped pecans in a food processor and grind until fine. Set the remaining 1½ cups aside.

Lightly but thoroughly grease a large, fluted tube pan. Carefully pour the finely ground pecans into the pan and rotate to coat the bottom.

TO PREPARE THE BATTER

Sift together the flour, baking powder, baking soda, salt and spices.

Cream the butter with the white and brown sugar until light. Add the eggs, one at a time, scraping the bowl well after each addition. Add the pumpkin, sour cream, molasses and dark rum. Add the dry ingredients and the remaining 1½ cups chopped pecans. Spread the batter into the prepared pan.

TO BAKE

Bake the cake in the preheated oven for approximately 1 hour and 15 minutes, or until a tester inserted into the center comes out clean. Cool the cake in the pan for 10 minutes, then carefully turn cake out onto a cooling rack to cool completely.

TO PREPARE THE SAUCE

When the cake has almost finished baking, prepare the sauce by combining all the ingredients together in a small saucepan. Bring to a rolling boil. Cool to warm.

Place the cake on the cooling rack, over a plate. Carefully pour the mixture over the cake, covering the top, allowing the glaze to dribble down the sides. Cool the cake to warm or room temperature before slicing.

THE GOOD TASTE

In poetry and prose runs one current theme –
The smell of new-baked bread is told with fervent zeal,
But I cling to the good delectable taste, I dream
Of a generous slice from a loaf's delicious, crunchy heel.

- Maude Rene Princehouse

HONEYED CORNBREAD

CORNBREAD BATTER

YIELD: 8 TO 12 SERVINGS

2 CUPS CORN MEAL

2 CUPS ALL-PURPOSE FLOUR

2 TEASPOONS SALT

2 TABLESPOONS
   PLUS 1 TEASPOON BAKING POWDER

2 CUPS MILK

½ CUP OIL

¾ CUP HONEY

3 EGGS

1 TABLESPOON VANILLA

Preheat the oven to 350 degrees.

CORNBREAD IN SEPTEMBER

When cornbread is fluffy and yellow
And covered with honey and butter,
Like sunshine all golden and mellow,
The heart of a small boy will flutter-
When cornbread is fluffy and yellow.

How often a man will remember
Its sweetness and long to recapture
The noons of a prairie September,
Bright hours when cornbread was rapture-
How often a man will remember!

- Grace V. Watkins

TO PREPARE THE PAN

Lightly grease a 9 inch by 13 inch pan.

TO PREPARE THE BATTER

Sift together the cornmeal, flour, salt and baking powder.

In another bowl, beat together the milk, oil, honey, eggs and vanilla.

Mix the wet ingredients with the dry just enough to moisten, being careful not to over-mix. The batter will be slightly lumpy. Pour the batter into the prepared pan.

TO BAKE

Bake in the fully preheated oven for 35 to 40 minutes, or until a toothpick inserted in the center comes out clean. Cool to warm before slicing. Spread with butter and drizzle with honey.

Wrap any leftovers in foil and reheat gently to serve at another time.

ROUNDELAY

Sweet to the settler was the mill-wheel's song,
[Prelude to progress to each new frontier]
A cheerful tune whose cadence all year long
Denied that threatened hunger could come near.

Sweet was the roundelay, endless the lilt
Of water-wheel and mill-race softly churning;
And endless were the towns and cities built
Around small mills where wheels were turning.

Through yesterday's old simple air became
A symphony, its audience world-wide,
Its melody, unchanged, is still the same
Fond hope of plenty through the countryside.

- Eloise Wade Hackett

CHAPTER FOUR

HOMEMADE YEAST ROLLS

DEDICATED TO THE PIONEER MILLING COMPANY

EST. 1851

THE PIONEER MILLING COMPANY

One hundred and fifty years ago, Carl Hilmar Guenther, an apprentice and millwright, at the age of 23, decided to leave his native country of Germany and come to America, the land of opportunity. He borrowed fifty dollars from a friend to pay for passage, and on May 5th, 1848, he boarded a ship with three hundred others on a fifty-six day voyage.

After arriving in New York, Mr. Guenther began traveling west. He was a man of many talents and skills and had little difficulty finding work. He was an expert in cabinet making and stone masonry and was versed in the production of power by steam through the use of the primitive machinery of his day. He also worked as farmer, miller and millwright.

His journey led him to the romantic and lovely little frontier village of San Antonio, Texas. About seventy-five miles to the northwest, in Fredericksburg, a small town had been established by a colony of German settlers in the heart of the Comanche country. This busy community of farmers, close to a convenient stream of water for power, was a town in need of a mill. Mr. Guenther decided he would build his first mill about nine miles west of Fredericksburg, on the banks of the Live Oak Creek.

With no tools other than pick and shovel, excavating the mill race and building a dam to impound the waters of Live Oak Creek were monumental undertakings. The water-wheel and driving gears were fashioned from native woods, and all were made on the spot in accordance with the designs drawn by Mr. Guenther. The sole exceptions were the millstones made in France of a special type of quartz found only in that country and brought up by ox-wagon through Indianola.

A typical southwest Texas flood rushed down upon the dam when it was near completion, swept it away and made necessary a new start from the ground up. The rebuilding was costly and the delay vexatious. Mr. Guenther's impatience for completion scarcely exceeded that of the women of Fredericksburg who longed for the opening of a mill that would relieve them of the tedious daily task of grinding corn for their families' daily bread.

Then, finally, after weary months of back-breaking toil and the gravest risks and uncertainty, the water was released into the race. There was an adequate fall and sufficient power, and, when the various moving parts were finally assembled, "they fit perfectly and ran like clock-work." The faith of C.H.Guenther in his project and in his skill was vindicated in this hour of triumph.

Two years of plentiful rains and good crops followed. The labors of construction had lessened, the labors of operation set in, and in the busy days that followed, Mr. Guenther's fortunes, which had reached a desperately low point during the months of construction, began to mend.

The farmers discovered they could grow wheat as well as corn in the new country, and soon, Mr. Guenther's restless impatience for better things asserted itself. He began deepening and widening his canal and installed a second water-wheel and machinery for the grinding of wheat, offering better service to his community. This effort, more than any other factor, probably accounts for the survival of this one little grist mill from among the scores that thrived in their day and now are only nostalgic memories.

A ROMANCE WITH BAKING

The site Mr. Guenther chose in San Antonio was a beautiful pecan-studded area inside a bend of the San Antonio River, less than a mile below the center of the city-the same site that for almost one hundred and fifty years has been the home to Guenther's Mills and the Pioneer Flour Mills of today.

SANDWICHES, ASSORTED

Wafer-thin, one-bite size,
Shaped like hearts or butterflies,
Spread with dainty, exotic mixtures
Of everything but the kitchen fixtures,
They're placed on lace on a crystal plate
And served for tea in Sunday state.
Hearty, generously whacked,
Whole, with the crunchy crust intact,
Thick with slabs of country ham,

With beef or cheese or home-made jam,
They're stowed in a lunch box for the hand
Of every workman in the land,
And schoolboys swinging on their way
Down every lane in the U.S.A.!

- Ethel Jacobson

PROPER BAKING PROCEDURES FOR YEAST ROLLS

Yeast rolls can benefit from the same principals used in making bread except for a few exceptions. These few exceptions are listed below. Information on yeast dough can be found under PROPER BAKING PROCE-DURES FOR BREADS on page 15.

PREPARING THE PAN

Line a half-sheet pan with parchment paper or lightly grease a baking sheet.

SHAPING THE ROLLS

There are a number of attractive ways to shape rolls. I usually decide the shape I want to give the dough after it has risen, depending on how it feels. There are many variables to the amount of moisture in the dough. The protein level in the flour, the size of the eggs added to the dough, the potato moisture content, the amount of time the dough was kneaded and so forth, all play key factors.

A softer dough might be divided and shaped round, then spaced close together when panned, while a firmer dough may be shaped into crescents or tied into knots and spaced further apart.

PANNING THE ROLLS

Pan the rolls close together for soft sides and further apart for firm.

PREHEATING THE OVEN

It is important the oven reaches the correct temperature before the rolls go in. Start preheating the oven right after the rolls have been shaped and panned, before they start their final rise.

EGG WASH

Egg wash, a mixture of an egg beaten with a tablespoon or two of water, can be applied to any of the roll recipes listed in this chapter just before they go into the oven. The egg wash, brushed on evenly, gives the rolls a rich golden color and helps any addition of nuts or seeds to adhere. The addition of oats, nuts, seeds, herbs or cheese should give hints of what is contained in the dough.

CHECKING FOR DONENESS

Rolls don't need to be baked long because of their size. A light golden brown color is sufficient for rolls spaced apart, while soft sided rolls, spaced close together, need to be a little darker. Be sure not to over-bake your rolls. They tend to dry out quickly.

REMEMBER

How we wrapped our stocking cap
Around, around, then turned the tassel in?
The mittens anchored to a cord
And the thick-ribbed hose pulled over shoes
And fastened with a pin?
The sharp hard wind, so bitter sweet,
Against chin, cheek and nose?
Snow angels blossoming against the hills
Where sled track patterns rose
Up to the red sun quickly falling –
The tingle in snow-bitten toes?
And then the call, the open door
The tightening hunger and the surging in;

The clumsey fingers grasping buttons
The warmth of fire on reddened skin;
The spicy odors from the kitchen range
That filled the room and swam within our souls?
And over all, the wafted lift,
The smell of gold, hot baking rolls!
Remember?

- Doris Barnett Roace

BUTTERFLAKE ROLLS

YIELD: 24 ROLLS

1 CUP MILK
1 TABLESPOON YEAST
¼ CUP WARM WATER
1 TABLESPOON SUGAR
2 CUPS ALL-PURPOSE FLOUR
3 TABLESPOONS BUTTER
¼ CUP SUGAR
1 EGG
1 TEASPOON SALT
2 CUPS ALL-PURPOSE FLOUR
3 TABLESPOONS BUTTER FOR BRUSHING

TO PREPARE THE DOUGH

In a small pan, scald the milk by heating it gently until tiny bubbles appear around the outside edge of the pan. Remove it from the heat. In a large bowl, dissolve the yeast in the warm water and sprinkle in the sugar. When the milk mixture has cooled to warm, add it to the yeast mixture along with the first 2 cups of flour. Beat in a continuous clockwise motion until smooth. Continue beating 100 strokes. Allow this sponge to rest until it starts to rise. Cream together the butter and the sugar, then add the egg. Add this mixture, along with the salt, to the sponge. Add enough of the remaining 2 cups of flour to make a kneadable dough. Turn the dough out onto a lightly floured board and knead until smooth and elastic. Place the dough into a lightly oiled bowl, turning once to oil the top. Let rise until doubled. While the dough is rising, prepare the pans by lightly greasing two 12 cup muffin tins.

TO SHAPE THE ROLLS

After the dough has doubled in volume, start preheating the oven to 350 degrees. On a lightly floured board, roll the dough into a long rectangle, measuring 12 inches by 24 inches, approximately one inch thick. "Slack the dough back" by lifting it gently to make sure it is not sticking to the board. Let the dough rest for a few minutes while you melt the butter. This step helps the dough to keep its shape after it is cut. Brush the slacked, rested dough with melted butter. Cut the dough in half and place one half evenly on top of the other. Cut this stack evenly in half again and stack the dough again on top. Cut the dough into 24 even pieces and place them, cut side down into the prepared pans, allowing them to fan open on top. Cover with clean tea towels and let the rolls rise until almost doubled in volume.

TO BAKE

Bake the rolls in the fully preheated oven for 15-20 minutes, or until they are slightly golden. Serve hot out of the oven with additional butter.

WHEAT FARM

Chartreuse and copper,
Yellow and green,
These are the colors
That liven the scene.
Off in the distance
The purpling hills
Dream of these acres
That Maytime instills
With the vigor of growing,
The valor of wheat,
"I smell fresh-baked rolls, ma
When do we eat?"

–Helen Maring

A VERY YOUNG MAN PROPOSES

He came to me and placed his hand
Upon mine, Oh so shyly!
He called me lovely, called me good.
He would not sit, but humbly stood,
All palpitant, before me;
Then, bowing, fell upon his knee
And scanned my face, as with inner fear,
Besought my eyes, questioning, near;
But no word could he utter.
And so I asked, "What is it dear?"
He bounded up to kiss my ear
In whispering "Rolls and butter."

- Kunigunde Duncan

MATRIMONIAL ROLLS

ROLL DOUGH

YIELD: 12 ROLLS

1 CUP MILK

½ CUP (2 STICKS) BUTTER, CUT INTO SMALL PIECES

¼ CUP SUGAR

1 TABLESPOON YEAST

¼ CUP WARM WATER (105-110 DEGREES)

3 EGGS

2 TEASPOONS SALT

5 CUPS ALL-PURPOSE FLOUR

ADDITIONAL MELTED BUTTER

TO PREPARE THE DOUGH

In a small pan, scald the milk by heating it gently until tiny bubbles appear around the outside edge of the pan. Stir in the butter and sugar to melt. Remove it from the heat and allow to cool.

In a glass measuring cup, sprinkle the yeast over the warm water and allow to sit until foamy. When the milk mixture has cooled to warm, pour it into a large bowl and beat in the eggs. Add the yeast mixture, the salt and enough of the flour to make a kneadable dough.

Turn the dough out onto a lightly floured board and knead until smooth and elastic. Place the dough into a lightly oiled bowl, turning once to oil the top. Let rise until doubled.

TO PREPARE THE PAN

Lightly grease a 9 inch by 13 inch pan.

TO SHAPE THE ROLLS

After the dough has doubled in volume, start preheating the oven to 350 degrees.

Punch the dough down and on a lightly floured board, briefly knead to work out any air bubbles. Divide the dough into 12 even pieces and shape into rolls, giving them a nice rounded top. Space evenly in the pan, cover with clean tea towel and let the rolls rise until almost doubled in volume.

TO BAKE

Bake the rolls in the fully preheated oven for 15-20 minutes, or until they are slightly golden and sound hollow when lightly tapped.

BREATHLESS ONION ROLLS

ONION ROLL DOUGH

1 recipe of BUTTERFLAKE ROLL DOUGH, located on page 148.

> ¼ CUP FINELY MINCED ONION
> 2 TABLESPOONS FRESH, FINELY MINCED PARSLEY
> 2 TABLESPOONS FRESH, FINELY MINCED DILL

TO PREPARE THE DOUGH

Prepare one recipe of BUTTERFLAKE ROLL DOUGH as described on page 148.

Just before you turn the dough out onto the board to knead, add the minced onion and the finely chopped herbs. Knead the dough on a lightly floured board until smooth and elastic and the herbs are evenly distributed throughout the dough. Place the dough into a lightly oiled bowl, turning once to oil the top. Let rise until almost doubled.

TO SHAPE AND PAN

Divide the dough into 12 even pieces and form into rounds or your favorite shape. Pan close together on a sheet pan lined with parchment paper, or on a lightly greased baking dish. Cover the rolls with a clean tea towel and let rise until almost doubled.

TO BAKE

While the rolls are rising, preheat the oven to 350 degrees. Bake the rolls in the fully preheated oven for 20-30 minutes, or until lightly golden. Brush with melted butter while hot.

SCOPE OF KITCHENS

Who talks about a kitchen's narrow scope,
Its menial tasks, has never stopped to think
What wonder-roads are worn from stove to sink,
What loveliness emanates from soap.
He has forgotten - in his deepest soul -
Romance in tea, the history in rice,
Geography in sugar, salt and spice,
The priceless perfume in a simple roll.

And more-that kitchens are the origin
Of poesy, of laughter, strength of men,
Of woman's grace; that pots and rolling-pin
Have motivated nations. Say not then
A kitchen's scope is limited, but sing:
Its glory transcends power of any king!

- Ethel Romig Fuller

WHOLE WHEAT BUTTERMILK ROLLS

154

YEILD: 12 ROLLS

Hot rolls make the butterfly!

- Mark Twain

ROLL DOUGH

1 CUP BUTTERMILK
½ CUP BUTTER (1 STICK)
⅓ CUP SUGAR
1 TABLESPOON YEAST
2 TO 2½ CUPS ALL-PURPOSE FLOUR
1 TEASPOON SALT
3 EGGS
2 CUPS WHOLE WHEAT FLOUR

TO PREPARE THE DOUGH

In a small saucepan, gently heat together the buttermilk, butter and the sugar until the butter melts. Cool to slightly warm. Sprinkle in the yeast and let set until foamy.

Beat in the eggs, then 2 cups of the all-purpose flour. Beat in a clockwise motion for two minutes. Let this sponge rest until it starts to rise.

Beat in the salt and the whole wheat flour. Pour out onto a floured board and knead until smooth and elastic, dusting the board from time to time with the remaining ½ cup of all-purpose flour to prevent the dough from sticking.

Shape into a ball and place into a clean, lightly oiled bowl, turning it once to lightly oil the top. Cover with a tea towel and let rise until doubled.

TO SHAPE AND BAKE THE ROLLS

Punch the dough down and knead briefly to remove any air bubbles. Let rest 10 minutes. Divide in half, then divide each half into 12 balls.

Arrange evenly spaced on 2 sheet pans that are lightly greased or lined with parchment paper.

Preheat the oven to 375 degrees.

Let the rolls rise until almost doubled. Bake in the fully preheated oven for 12 to 15 minutes, or until lightly golden.

MOTHER'S POTATO ROLLS

YIELD: 12 ROLLS

ROLL DOUGH

3 MEDIUM POTATOES

1 CUP MILK

1 (6 OUNCE) CAN MILK

1 CUP SUGAR

⅔ CUP (1½ STICKS) BUTTER,
   CUT INTO SMALL PIECES

2 TABLESPOONS YEAST

1 CUP ALL-PURPOSE FLOUR

2 EGGS

5 TO 6 CUPS ALL-PURPOSE FLOUR

EGG WASH AND SEED TOPPING

1 EGG

2 TABLESPOONS WATER

¼ CUP SESAME SEEDS

¼ CUP POPPY SEEDS

TO PREPARE THE DOUGH

Scrub and peel the potatoes. Cut them into small pieces and cook them in a small saucepan, covered with water until soft. Drain and mash them until smooth.

In a small pan, scald the milk by heating it gently until tiny bubbles appear around the outside edge of the pan. Pour the milk into a large bowl and add the butter and sugar. Stir to melt and allow to cool to warm.

When the potatoes have cooled to warm, add them, along with the yeast to the cooled milk mixture. Stir in one cup of the white flour and beat until smooth. Continue to beat in a continuous clockwise direction for 100 strokes. Let this sponge rest until light and foamy.

Beat in the 2 eggs and enough of the remaining flour to make a kneadable dough. Pour the dough out onto a floured board and knead well until smooth and elastic. Place the dough into a lightly oiled bowl, turning it once to lightly oil the top. Cover with a clean tea towel and let rise until almost doubled in volume, about 1 hour.

Line a half-sheet pan with parchment paper or lightly grease a baking sheet.

Preheat the oven to 350 degrees. Punch the dough down and knead briefly to work out any air bubbles. Divide the rolls into 12 even pieces. Shape the rolls, giving them smooth tops. Evenly space them, sides touching, into a circle. Cover and let rise until almost doubled in volume.

EGG WASH

Beat together the egg and water. After the rolls have almost doubled in volume, lightly brush them with egg wash. Sprinkle sesame seeds on one half of the circle and the poppy seeds on the other. Bake the rolls in the fully preheated oven for 15-20 minutes, or until they are slightly golden and sound hollow when lightly tapped.

TIE THE KNOT CHEESE KNOTS

YEILD: 12 ROLLS

1 recipe of BUTTERFLAKE ROLL DOUGH, located on page 148.

2 CUPS GRATED CHEDDAR CHEESE
1 CUP GRATED SWISS CHEESE

TO PREPARE THE DOUGH

Prepare one recipe of BUTTERFLAKE ROLL DOUGH, eliminating the butter for brushing from the list of ingredients.

Just before you turn the dough out onto the board to knead, add the grated cheddar and Swiss cheese. Knead the dough until smooth and elastic.

Place the dough into a lightly oiled bowl, turning once to lightly oil the top. Cover with a tea towel and let rise until doubled.

TO PREPARE THE PAN

Line a half sheet pan with parchment paper or lightly grease a baking sheet.

Punch the dough down and knead briefly to work out any air bubbles. Divide the dough into 14 even pieces. Roll each piece into an 8" rope by gently rolling it back and forth with your hands on a lightly floured board. Tie each rope into a knot and pinch the ends together. Place the knots, pinched seam side down, onto the prepared pan, spaced evenly apart to give them room to rise. Cover with a clean tea towel and let rise until almost doubled. Preheat the oven to 350 degrees.

TO BAKE

Bake the knots in the fully preheated oven for 20 minutes or until golden. Cool slightly before serving.

MAY DAY EXCHANGE

She knew that he would come at dusk,
A May basket in his hand,
Brimming with blossoms pink and white,
The loveliest in the land.
Smiling, she took the flowers and versed
In matrimonial goals,
Gave back the basket filled with a dozen
Fragrant home-made rolls.

- Grace V. Watkins

WONDERFUL BRAN ROLLS

YIELD: 24 ROLLS

½ CUP (1 STICK) BUTTER,
  CUT INTO SMALL PIECES
⅓ CUP SUGAR
½ CUP BRAN
¾ TEASPOON SALT
½ CUP BOILING WATER
1 TABLESPOON DRY YEAST
½ CUP WARM WATER
1 EGG
3 CUPS ALL-PURPOSE FLOUR

PORTRAIT OF GREAT-AUNT LIZA

Up in the attic, tucked away
In a dusty box, I found, today,
An odd little bonnet of plush and jet -
Great-Aunt Liza's...I see her yet
In the scrap of bonnet, and plain dark gown
On the shadowed streets of our country town,
Bearing a basket deep and wide,
Scores of her home-made rolls inside
To hearten the ill, or those in need
Of a friendly thought and a gracious deed.
Sickness and sorrow, she always said,
Deserved the best, be it love or bread.
We know, who recall her last slow pace,
That Great-Aunt Liza walks in grace.

- Sadie Fuller Seagrave

TO PREPARE THE DOUGH

Put the cut up butter, sugar, bran and the salt into a large mixing bowl and pour the boiling water over it. Stir the mixture to melt the butter, then cool.

In a separate small bowl, sprinkle the yeast over the warm water to dissolve.

When the bran mixture has cooled to warm, pour the yeast mixture into the bran and beat in the egg and the flour.

Pour the dough out onto a lightly floured board and knead until smooth and elastic. Place the dough into a lightly oiled bowl and turn once to oil the top. Cover with a clean tea towel and let rise until doubled.

TO PREPARE THE PANS

Generously grease two 12 cup muffin pans.

Punch the dough down and knead briefly to work out any air bubbles. Divide the dough into 24 even pieces. With lightly oiled fingers, shape the pieces into round rolls, giving them smooth, rounded tops. Place the rolls into the prepared pans.

Cover the rolls with a clean tea towel and let rise until almost doubled.

While the rolls are rising, preheat the oven to 350 degrees.

Bake the rolls in the fully preheated 350 degrees oven for 15 minutes, or until golden brown. Cool slightly, then remove from the pans and serve hot with butter.

SPINNAKER ROLLS

YEILD: 12 ROLLS

SPINNAKER ROLL DOUGH

1 recipe of BUTTERFLAKE ROLL DOUGH, located on page 148.

2 CUPS GRATED CHEDDAR CHEESE
1 SMALL CAN (4 OUNCES) DRAINED, MILD,
CHOPPED JALAPEÑO PEPPERS

TO PREPARE THE DOUGH

Prepare one recipe of BUTTERFLAKE ROLL DOUGH as described on page 148. Turn the dough out onto a lightly floured board and knead until smooth and elastic. Place the dough into a lightly oiled bowl, turning once to oil the top. Let rise until doubled.

After the dough has doubled in volume, punch the dough down and add the grated cheddar cheese and the jalapeño   peppers. Knead the dough on a lightly floured board to distribute the cheese and peppers evenly.

TO SHAPE AND PAN THE ROLLS

Lightly grease a 9 inch by 13 inch pan. Divide the dough into 12 even pieces and shape into rolls, giving them a nice rounded top. Space evenly in the pan, cover with clean tea towel and let the rolls rise until almost doubled in volume.

TO BAKE

While the rolls are rising, preheat the oven to 350 degrees. Bake the rolls in the fully preheated oven for 15-20 minutes, or until lightly golden. Brush with melted butter while hot.

DINAH KNEADING DOUGH

I have seen full many a sight
Born of day or drawn by night:
Sunlight on a silver stream,
Golden lilies all a-dream,
Lofty mountains, bold and proud,
Veiled beneath the lace-like cloud;
But no lovely sight I know
Equals Dinah kneading dough.

Brown arms buried elbow-deep
Their romantic rhythm keep,
As with steady sweep they go
Through the gently yielding dough.
Maids may vaunt their finer charms –
Naught to me like Dinah's arms;
Girls may draw, or paint, or sew –
I love Dinah kneading dough.

Eyes of jet and teeth of pearl,
Hair, some say, to tight a-curl;
But the dainty maid I deem
Very near perfection's dream.
Swift she works, and only flings
Me a glance – the least of things.
And I wonder, does she know
That my heart is in the dough?

Candle Lightin' Time 1901

THE MILL WHEEL

By the shadowed waters cool and green,
The old mill mutely stands;
The fresh young saplings toward it lean,
With plumed, caressing hands.
The empty windows frame no face,
The rotting wheel is still
That once was whirled with merry pace,
By waters 'neath the mill.

The waning glow of soft spring day,
Plays on the crumbling walls;
Wee owlets on the rafters sway,
As darkness softly falls.
The twilight wind slips gently through,
Stirring the sleeping dust,
Mingling with fragrant scented dew,
Odors of mold and must.

'Tis said by those who've watched before,
When stars are overhead,
A shape glides through the creaking door,
With old, familiar tread.
The gaunt mill shakes with sudden sobs–
An aftermath of pain;
From the water's edge comes a steady throb–
The mill wheel turns again!

- Neil Lanier Garrett

CHAPTER FIVE

ENTICING TARTS

DEDICATED TO THE MORRISON MILLING COMPANY

EST. 1886

THE MORRISON MILLING COMPANY

The Morrison Milling Company of Denton, Texas, is Texas' second-oldest mill. Founded by North Texas area farmers in 1886 as a cooperative venture, the mill was first known as the Farmers' Alliance Milling Company. The farmers, unable to mill their own wheat and corn individually, joined together to establish their own independent mill to provide for the baking needs of the Denton area. Farmers' Alliance Milling Company was one of the first agrarian cooperatives in the country.

Within a few years, the mill was sold to a group of local businessmen. The venture proved successful. By the turn of the century, the firm had already won so many first awards for its premium flour that it was barred from further competition at the State Fair in Texas. In 1900, Alliance Milling Company received worldwide recognition by winning the First Prize Gold Medal at the Paris International Exposition.

Excellent flour, however, was not enough to make the mill thrive. In 1916, a dramatic change in the wheat market forced the sale of the mill for a second time. The milling company maintained a sound financial footing through the First World War, but a decade or more of losses followed. What was needed, it seemed, was the guidance of someone with an extensive knowledge of the larger business world as well as the milling industry.

E. Walter Morrison, Sr., appeared to be just the man. When he left Kansas in 1936 to purchased the Alliance Milling Company, the company had only a handful of customers, local distribution of products, and deteriorating equipment and facilities. The mill was almost idle. The mill changed hands to become The Morrison Milling Company, and the downward trend soon reversed. Morrison's previous experience and network of contacts in the milling business helped bring in a modest profit within a year after the mill's acquisition.

By broadening the mill's market to the east coast and even Holland prior to World War II, Morrison put it on a firm financial foundation. With the advent of the war, the mill became the supplier to the military installations across the region. Post-war prosperity continued for the mill through the 1940's, and by 1950 the grain storage elevators had reached capacity and expansion was necessary.

At this time, Morrison resumed establishing markets away from its immediate area. The mill began shipping products to other southern cities and resumed international distribution, selling flour and meal to Europe and the Caribbean countries. Products were sold as far away as Central and South America.

A completed renovation and expansion to the 100 year old mill brought installation of state-of-the-art equipment. New technology enabled the mill to more than double its daily capacity without additional floor space.

Today, the addition of its "Kit Family" of products has allowed Morrison to expand its products to a more diversified retail consumer. The original three mixes, Corn-Kits, Bis-Kits and Pan-Kits, has been broadened to now include fourteen members. Additionally, a full line of food service mixes has been developed to compliment its retail and bakery flour items. Customized service and products continue to allow Morrison Milling Company to increase its market share.

215

I AM THE QUEEN

I have no voice to sing-nor can I write –
For o'er my shoulder muses won't indite.
But in my little home I lift my head
And praise god for my skill in making bread.
Fresh from the oven, fragrant, brown and light,
My heart rejoices at the tempting sight.

I envy no one and I cease to dread
Life's hardships - for I know I can make bread.
The queens of modern times that diamonds wear,
Who dwell in mansions feted everywhere,
Surpass me not. When all is done and said,
I am the queen-because I make the bread.

— Susan Hubbard Martin

PROPER BAKING PROCEDURES FOR TARTS

There are four different types of tart dough featured in this chapter. Two of them contain procedures within the recipe. One is a roll-out crust and the same principals and techniques are used as in the preparation of pie dough, see PROPER BAKING PROCEDURES FOR PIES, page 194. The other crust in this chapter is a shortbread that is pressed into shape. For the shortbread tart dough:

WORKING WITH THE TART DOUGH

When preparing the shortbread tart dough, have the butter at room temperature or put it in a microwave for a few seconds until it is soft, but not melted.

TO LINE THE TART PANS

The shortbread crust recipe featured makes two tart crusts. The recipe calls for two 10 inch round, fluted pans with removable bottoms. Divide the tart dough evenly between the two pans and press it into the sides, than evenly onto the bottom of the two 10 inch rounds. Gently press your thumb around the inside edges to smooth out the dough. Wrap one tart in plastic wrap and store in the freezer for another occasion, or double the tart filling recipe and fill both crusts to make two tarts.

BAKING THE CRUST BLIND

This shortbread crust keeps its shape in the oven. If you are making a chocolate or cream filled tart, pre-bake the tart on a sheet pan in the oven until lightly golden, then cool completely before filling.

REMOVING THE TART FROM THE PAN

If the tart shell is to be filled after it is baked, allow it to cool before filling. Then, allow the filling to set before removing from the pan. If the tart is baked with the filling, after it is baked, allow the tart and filling to cool in the pan before removing the rim. This will help the sides of the tart to set.

If the filled, baked tart bubbles over when baked and sticks to the side of the pan, after it has cooled, set the tart in the hot oven for a minute or two to warm it up slightly, then carefully lift it out of the pan.

Lift the tart up from the center to remove the rim. Place the tart on a flat surface, then carefully slide a knife under the tart to release it from the pan. Carefully slide it onto a large, flat, pretty plate or cake board (see page 223). Cut into wedges to serve.

HAVING EYES TO SEE

As I went walking out at morn
I saw a twisted blackberry thorn;
I saw the grain dashed by the wind,
And three stark trees on a gray sky lined.
"What did you do this dawning, boy,
And was there ought to give you joy?"
I found more joy than I could tell,
Two bees swung in a hollyhock bell;
A foamy sea of clover bloom
Had rainbow dew and a spider's loom.
Then a fragrance made me turn away...
My mother's baking a tart today.

- Charlene Underwood

CHOCOLATE TRUFFLE HEARTS

YIELD: 8 TO 12 SERVINGS

SHORTBREAD TART CRUST

1 recipe, located on page 186.

FILLING

1¾ CUPS HEAVY CREAM
15 OUNCES GOOD QUALITY, FINELY CHOPPED CHOCOLATE

GARNISH

1 PINT FRESH RASPBERRIES
FRESH MINT SPRIGS

TO PREPARE THE CRUST

Prepare one recipe of SHORTBREAD TART DOUGH, following the directions on page 186. Press the dough evenly to cover the bottom and up the sides of six to eight heart shaped tart shells, preferably with removable bottoms. Or, you can prepare this tart in an 8 or 10 inch tart pan. Prepare the dough as described, then wrap one unbaked shell in plastic wrap and freeze for another time, or double the filling recipe and make two tarts.

TO BAKE THE CRUST OR CRUSTS

Preheat the oven to 350 degrees. Place the unbaked shell or shells on a baking sheet and bake in the fully preheated oven for 5-10 minutes (depending on the size of your pans) or until the tart shell starts to turn lightly golden. Remove from the sheet pan and cool completely in the tins. Leave in the tins until serving time.

TO PREPARE THE FILLING

Bring the heavy cream to a boil. While the cream is heating, chop the chocolate and place it in a large stainless steel bowl. Pour the hot cream over the chopped chocolate and whisk until smooth. Pour the filling into the prepared tart shell or shells. Chill until set, or overnight.

TO UNMOLD AND GARNISH

After the tart or tarts have cooled completely and are set, unmold them and garnish with fresh raspberries and mint.

ROMANTIC PATTERN

A recent article in reference
To young men's matrimonial preference
Informs us that tarts, cake and pie
Are very pleasing to the eye,
While signs of culinary zeal
Would seem to have a marked appeal.
[And I suspect the same holds true
With men of riper ages too!]

- Grace V. Watkins

FRESH FALL PEAR TART

YIELD: 8 TO 12 SERVINGS

SHORTBREAD TART DOUGH

1 recipe, located on page 186.

FILLING

⅔ CUP SUGAR

3 TABLESPOONS ALL-PURPOSE FLOUR

2 EGGS, LIGHTLY BEATEN

6 TABLESPOONS BUTTER, MELTED AND COOLED

1 TEASPOON ALMOND EXTRACT

¼ CUP GROUND ALMONDS (OPTIONAL)

2 BARTLETT PEARS

AUTUMN MELODY

Autumn is a melody –
A rhythm of swaying leaves,
The music of an eager wind
Turning the restless sheaves;
The hum of motors strikes a chord,
From across a golden field
As men and engines chant loud praise
For this golden yield,
Autumn is a bold, bright melody,
Sung in unison,
A song to sing while working,
And to remember when work is done.

–Rosalie Barnett Spindler

TO PREPARE THE CRUST

Prepare one recipe of SHORTBREAD TART DOUGH, following the directions on page 186. Place one unbaked shell in plastic wrap and freeze for another time, or double the filling recipe and make two tarts. Place the unbaked shell or shells on a baking sheet and set aside.

Preheat the oven to 350 degrees.

TO PREPARE THE FILLING

In a small saucepan over low heat, gently melt the butter. Cool. Blend the sugar and flour together in a mixing bowl. Beat in the eggs until light. Add the melted, cooled butter and gradually beat it into the egg mixture. Add the almond extract and blend well.

Peel, core and thinly slice the pears and arrange them in a pretty, slightly overlapping, circular pattern in the prepared shell. Carefully and slowly pour the filling evenly over the pears. Sprinkle the ground almonds around the outer edge is desired.

TO BAKE THE TART

Bake the tart in the fully preheated oven for 40 to 45 minutes or until it starts to puff up slightly, turns lightly golden and the center is set. Serve warm or at room temperature.

MOST CORDIAL FRESH RASPBERRY TART

YIELD: 8 SERVINGS

TART CRUST

1 CUP BUTTER

1 CUP BROWN SUGAR

1 EGG

½ TEASPOON VANILLA

2 CUPS ALL-PURPOSE FLOUR

½ TEASPOON BAKING POWDER

½ TEASPOON SALT

½ CUP GROUND ALMONDS

FILLING

1 CUP SUGAR

¾ CUP COLD WATER

2½ TABLESPOONS CORN STARCH

¼ TEASPOON SALT

RASPBERRIES

GRANDMOTHER'S BAKING

The smell of goods baking is almost soulshaking
When Grandmother's baking comes to mind.
Her raspberry tart would melt stony hearts –
Ambrosia and nectar combined.

Her apple and mince could almost convince
A sinner to live as he should,
While her lemon meringue shot an envious pang
Through neighbors whose weren't as good.

The kitchen was fragrant with many a vagrant
Aroma that made your mouth water,
It was Grandma's career and how she would jeer
At the pies of her lazy granddaughter;
For I'd rather spend time at writing a rhyme
[For which I hope to get paid]
Even though I disgrace my grandmother's race
By buying my tarts ready made.

- Eloise Wade Hackett

TO PREPARE THE CRUST

Cream together the butter and sugar. Add the egg and vanilla and beat until incorporated. Sift together the flour, baking powder and salt and add it to the creamed mixture. Add the ground almonds and mix well.

Spread this mixture onto a piece of waxed paper, then place another piece of waxed paper over the top and carefully roll the dough between the two sheets into a circle, slightly larger than your pan. Chill the dough well.

TO PREPARE THE PAN

Line a 10 inch tart or cake pan with parchment paper by tracing a circle around the pan and cutting it to fit. If you are using a pan with a removable bottom, no preparation is necessary.

Carefully peel the top paper off the chilled dough, flip it over and center it over the prepared pan. Press it gently onto the bottom, into the corners and up the sides. (Depending on the size of your pan, you may have a little extra dough.) Flute the edges. If the dough gets sticky, chill for a few more minutes. Chill while you preheat the oven to 350 degrees.

TO BAKE THE CRUST

Bake the crust in the fully preheated oven until it starts to turn light in color, but is not quite set, about ten to 15 minutes. Run a spoon gently around the inside edge to keep the sides in shape. Bake again until the tart rim is very lightly golden. Cool while you prepare the filling.

TO PREPARE THE FILLING

Sort through the berries, saving the prettiest ones for the top. Whisk together in a saucepan the cold water, sugar, cornstarch and salt. Add any less than perfect berries (you'll need one cup), to the cornstarch mixture and bring to a boil, whisking often to keep from sticking.

ASSEMBLING THE TART

Cool the filling to warm, then pour the filling into the pre-baked, cooled crust, being careful not to overfill. Arrange the raspberries, open side down, in a circular pattern into the filling, starting with the outer edge. Fill in the rest, spacing them close together, until the tart is covered. Chill until set or overnight.

DAINTY LEMON CURD TART

YIELD: 8 TO 12 SERVINGS

SHORTBREAD TART CRUST

1 recipe, located on page 186.

FILLING

½ CUP (1 STICK) BUTTER
1 TABLESPOON FRESH GRATED LEMON ZEST
½ CUP FRESH LEMON JUICE
1½ CUPS SUGAR
5 EGGS, BEATEN

GARNISH

2 CUPS WHIPPING CREAM
FRESH LEMON SLICES
FRESH MINT SPRIGS

TARTS

"There's tarts for supper," mother said
And took them from the tin.
The plate was at the table's edge
Where I could rest my chin.

I watched the glow of lemon jell'
On rounds of gold brown crust,
Then mother slipped the covers on
And sprinkled sugar dust.

"There's one too many for the plate,"
I said, and as if planned
She lifted up the biggest tart
And put it in my hand.

- Marion Woodall

TO PREPARE THE CRUST

Prepare one recipe of SHORTBREAD TART DOUGH, following the directions on page 186.

TO BAKE THE CRUST

Preheat the oven to 350 degrees. Place the unbaked shell or shells on a baking sheet and bake in the fully preheated oven approximately 10 minutes, or until the tart shell starts to turn lightly golden. Remove from the sheet pan and cool completely in the tin. Leave in the tin until serving time.

TO PREPARE THE FILLING

In a medium size saucepan, on low heat, melt the butter. Add the fresh lemon zest, fresh lemon juice and the sugar. Cook, stirring until the sugar dissolves, then remove from the heat. Whisking constantly, beat in the eggs. Return the mixture to the stove and cook over low heat, until thick and starts to bubble, about 10-15 minutes. Cool to warm. Fill the pre-baked, cooled crust. Chill completely in the refrigerator until set.

TO UNMOLD AND GARNISH

After the tart has cooled completely and is set, unmold the tart onto a pretty serving plate. Whip the whipping cream until slightly stiff. Gently score the tart with the number of desired servings. With a star pastry tip and pastry bag, pipe a swirled mound of whipped cream on each serving. Garnish with the fresh lemon and mint.

PLUM STREUSEL TART

YIELD: 6 TO 8 SERVINGS

SHORTBREAD TART CRUST

1 recipe, located on page 186.

TART FILLING

5-6 CUPS PITTED AND SLICED PLUMS
¼ CUP ALL-PURPOSE FLOUR
1 CUP SUGAR
1 TEASPOON CINNAMON
½ TEASPOON NUTMEG

STREUSEL TOPPING

½ CUP (1 STICK) COLD BUTTER
½ CUP ALL-PURPOSE FLOUR
½ CUP BROWN SUGAR
1 TEASPOON CINNAMON
½ CUP CHOPPED WALNUTS

TO PREPARE THE CRUST

Prepare one recipe of SHORTBREAD TART DOUGH, following the directions on page 186, using a 8 inch by 3 inch deep-dish tart pan. Line another small tart tin with the remaining dough, wrap it in plastic and freeze to use at another time. Place the unbaked shell onto a sheet pan and set aside.

TO PREPARE THE FILLING

Wash and remove the pits from the plums. Slice plums into a large bowl. In another bowl, mix together the flour, sugar, cinnamon and nutmeg. Toss the plums with this mixture to coat well. Turn the plums into the prepared pastry shell, sprinkling any remaining sugar mixture over the top.

TO PREPARE THE STREUSEL TOPPING

Cut the cold butter into small pieces and place into a food processor. Add the flour, brown sugar and the cinnamon. Process briefly until the mixture resembles coarse meal. Add the chopped walnuts and process briefly again. Be sure not to over process! The mixture should remain crumbly. Pile the streusel topping onto the top of the tart.

TO BAKE

Bake the tart on the sheet pan or baking sheet in a fully preheated 350 degree oven for approximately 1 hour, or until the tart filling starts to bubble and the crumb topping starts to turn golden brown. Remove from the sheet pan and cool to warm before removing from the pan or serving.

TREASURED BUTTERSCOTCH PECAN TART

180

YIELD: 8 TO 10 SERVINGS

WONDERFUL TART CRUST

1 recipe, located on page 186.

TART FILLING

4 EGGS
1½ CUPS + 2 TBS. WHITE SUGAR
1½ CUPS DARK CORN SYRUP
½ TEASPOON SALT
1 TEASPOON VANILLA
4 TBS. BUTTER, MELTED AND COOLED
5 OUNCES PECAN HALVES

GARNISH

WHIPPING CREAM, IF DESIRED

COUNTRY SPRINGTIME

Two beautiful things that fitly go together,
That are of country springtime mask and mark –
More lovely after the gloom of winter weather –
Are an emerald wheatfield and a meadowlark.
The bird, a gleam of sunshine, soars to sing
Above the shimmering wheat, his fluty strain
Spills shining from the bulging bins of spring,
Fortelling harvest time and ripened grain.

Happier goes the passer on his way,
Blessed and heartened by that springtime sight:
The golden bird fluting his roundelay,
The field so green, lit by a lambent light.
Seeing this miracle, this thing so fair,
Even the sad heart quits awhile its care.

- Maude Rene Princehouse

TO PREPARE THE TART CRUST

Prepare one recipe of WONDERFUL TART DOUGH, following the directions on page 186.

Roll the dough out on a lightly floured board to fit a 10 inch, removable bottom tart pan. Gently place the tart dough into the pan, fitting the dough into the corners and gently pressing the dough into the fluted sides. Press your thumb around the top edge to remove any excess dough. Prick the bottom with a fork.

TO PREPARE THE FILLING

Beat together the eggs, sugar, dark corn syrup, salt, vanilla and the melted, cooled butter. Pour into the unbaked tart shell and cover the top in a circular pattern with the pecan halves.

TO BAKE THE TART

Place the tart on a half sheet pan or a cookie sheet to catch any butter that seeps out during the baking process. Bake in the preheated oven for 10 to 15 minutes, then turn the oven down to 300 degrees and bake until set. Cool to warm before serving. Serve with dollops of freshly whipped cream.

LUSCIOUS APPLE TART

YIELD: 8 TO 10 SERVINGS

CRUST

2 CUPS ALL-PURPOSE FLOUR
⅔ CUP SUGAR
½ CUP BROWN SUGAR
2 TEASPOONS VANILLA
1 CUP (2 STICKS) COLD BUTTER

TOPPING

1 TEASPOON CINNAMON
½ CUP SUGAR
3 TO 4 LARGE GRANNY SMITH APPLES
½ CUP SLICED ALMONDS

FILLING

1½ POUNDS CREAM CHEESE, SOFTENED
1 CUP SUGAR
1 TABLESPOON VANILLA
3 EGGS

TO PREPARE THE CRUST

Toss together in a mixing bowl the flour, sugar, brown sugar and vanilla. Cut the butter into small pieces and add, mixing on low speed until it resembles coarse meal. To keep the crust tender be sure not to over-mix. (If you like you can cut the butter in with a pastry cutter.) Press the dough softly into a 9 inch spring form pan, building the sides up 1 inch.

TO PREPARE THE FILLING

Thoroughly beat together the cream cheese, sugar and the vanilla. Add the eggs, one at a time, scraping the bottom of the bowl after each addition. Carefully pour the filling into the prepared crust.

Preheat the oven to 350 degrees while you prepare the topping.

TO PREPARE THE TOPPING

In a medium size bowl, toss together the cinnamon and sugar. Cut the apples in half, cut each half into five sections. Peel them, then toss them into the cinnamon sugar mixture to coat and arrange them on top of the cream cheese filling in a circular pattern to cover.

TO BAKE THE TART

Place the tart on a sheet pan or cookie sheet with sides to catch any butter that seeps out, and bake in the preheated oven for about 50 minutes or until the tart feels slightly firm to the touch. Remove from the oven and sprinkle with the sliced almonds. Bake for another 10-15 minutes or until the almonds are lightly toasted and the tart is set, or when a knife inserted in the center comes out clean. Serve warm or cold.

BLUEBERRY ALMOND CRUMB TART

184

FIELD: 8 TO 10 SERVINGS

SHORTBREAD TART DOUGH

1 recipe, located on page 186.

ALMOND FILLING

1½ CUPS SLICED ALMONDS
¾ CUP SUGAR
½ CUP BUTTER, ROOM TEMPERATURE
1 EGG
1 TABLESPOON ALL-PURPOSE FLOUR
1 TEASPOON VANILLA
3 CUPS FRESH BLUEBERRIES

CRUMB TOPPING

¾ CUP (1½ STICKS) COLD BUTTER
¾ CUP ALL-PURPOSE FLOUR
¾ CUP BROWN SUGAR
1½ TEASPOONS CINNAMON
½ CUP SLICED ALMONDS

He thinks of everything…
who wants his tart now.

- English saying

Preheat the oven to 350 degrees.

TO PREPARE THE CRUST

Prepare one recipe of SHORTBREAD TART DOUGH, following the directions on page 186. Gently press it evenly into a ¼ inch thick shell on the bottom and 1½ inches up the sides of a 10 inch spring form cake pan. Line a small tart tin with the remaining dough. Wrap the small tart shell in plastic and freeze to use at another time. Place the unbaked shell onto a sheet pan and set aside.

TO PREPARE THE ALMOND FILLING

Finely grind the almonds with the sugar in a food processor. Add the butter, egg, flour and vanilla and process briefly again to mix well. Spread the almond filling into the prepared crust. Top the almond filling with the blueberries.

TO PREPARE THE CRUMB TOPPING

Cut the cold butter into small pieces and place into a food processor. Add the flour, brown sugar and the cinnamon. Process briefly until the mixture resembles coarse meal. Add the almonds and process briefly again. Be sure not to over process! The mixture should remain crumbly. Pile the streusel topping onto the top of the tart.

TO BAKE

Bake the tart on the sheet pan or baking sheet in the fully preheated oven for about 1 hour, or until the tart crust starts to turn golden and the filling is set around the edges. A knife inserted into the center should come out clean. Remove from the sheet pan and cool to warm before removing from the pan or serving. Serve warm or at room temperature.

SHORTBREAD TART CRUST

YIELD: 2 CRUSTS

¾ CUP (1½ STICKS) SOFT, (NOT MELTED) BUTTER
2 CUPS ALL-PURPOSE FLOUR
3 TABLESPOONS SUGAR
2 EGG YOLKS

Put the butter in a microwave for a few seconds until it is soft, but not melted.

In a mixing bowl, blend the flour and the sugar. Add the butter to the flour mixture to blend. Add the egg yolks and mix thoroughly.

Divide the tart dough evenly between two 10 inch round, fluted pans with removable bottoms. Press this mixture evenly into the sides and then the bottom. Wrap one tart in plastic wrap and store in the freezer for another occasion, or double the tart filling recipe and fill both crusts to make two tarts.

WONDERFUL TART CRUST

1 CUP ALL-PURPOSE FLOUR
1 TABLESPOON SUGAR
½ CUP (1 STICK) COLD BUTTER
1 EGG

TO PREPARE THE CRUST

Mix the flour with the sugar. With a pastry cutter, cut in the butter until it resembles coarse meal. Add the eggs and mix the dough until it forms a ball. Knead briefly until smooth.

Roll out into a circle on a lightly floured board. Gently place the dough into the tart pan, easing it into the corners. Trim the excess from the top by smoothing it with your thumb.

This recipe makes enough tart dough to fill a 9 inch deep tart pan or a 10 inch flat tart pan.

DOUGH IN THE PAN

When I was a young girl my mother taught me how to make good bread:
"Be sure, my dear, you scrape the dough clean from the pan," she said
And I would work the flour in until the pan would shine,
Freed from dough, and I was proud of that task of mine.
My mother told me of a Prince whose riding horse went lame;
Of how he toured the countryside, and at every door he came
Asking for dough left in the pans to heal the injured leg,
But of many a pretty lass he had no need to beg.
Eager they were to serve the Prince with hands full of waste dough,
But the Prince was seeking for a bride that far day long ago.
He would not have a wasted wife and he sought and searched for long
Until he stopped at a humble cottage and heard a lifted song
Where a happy maiden was mixing bread beside an open door,
And the Prince alighted and made the same request he had made before.
"But Sir," she said, "I never leave the least dough in the pan..."
And the pleased Prince smiled and said to himself: Here's a wife for a man."
And as I worked my flour in when I was a girl, thought I
Perhaps this will be the beautiful day when a Prince comes riding by!

– Grace Noll Crowell

AN OLD MILL

I'm thinking of an old mill
Where purple passion vines
Screen a partly fallen wall
And wild-rose interwine.

The way's through scented meadows,
Over a hill and down,
Below a cliff, beside a stream,
Within a the sight of town.

It's lovely there in Autumn
When the goldenrod is bright,
And multicolored butterflies
Are twinkling in the light.

And when the landscape's softened
By twilight's magic spell,
I hear again the creaking wheel–
The sound I love so well.

- Edwin B. McElfatrick

CHAPTER SIX

OLD FASHIONED PIES

DEDICATED TO THE LACEY MILLING COMPANY

EST. 1887

LACEY MILLING COMPANY

192

No local industry or firm is more intimately identified with the early development of Hanford, California, than the Lacey Milling Company. In the declining years of the last century, when the state was young and wheat was the only game in town for most of the Valley farmers, the local grain and feed mill was as much a part of the community life as the bank and the barber shop.

The family business began in 1857, during the turbulent days before the Civil War, when 22 year old Horatio G. Lacey moved west to Fort Scott, Kansas, and became acquainted with the grist mill business. It was there that he erected a flour and saw mill which he operated for nearly 20 years.

After marrying, the lure of the West brought him to Visalia, California, where the Massachusetts native became involved in mechanical engineering, the running of threshing and farm machinery, and milling.

In 1887, H.G. Lacey was hired by J.H. Johnson, to manage his steam powered flour mill in Hanford, which was then the heart of the grain fields of western Tulare County. Lacey modernized and improved the plant's capacity to mill wheat and other grains raised on the surrounding lands by switching the mill's power source from steam to electricity. In 1892, he and his three sons, Loren, Ora, and Richard purchased the Hanford Flour Mill from the original owner and operated it as the H.G. Lacey Company.

The mill's early growth coincided with the boom of vast wheat ranches owned by the grain and cattle barons who controlled much of the Valley's rich farm land. While six million bushels of wheat were harvested statewide in 1860, 40 million bushels were raised in 1889, much of it for export to England and other European countries.

In April of 1916, while the country was embroiled in World War I, the original wooden Hanford Mill was destroyed by fire. It was rebuilt, modernized, and reopened in November of that year under the name of H.G. Lacey Milling Company. The mill and much of the equipment installed after the fire are still in operation.

Today the mill specializes in milling tortilla flour for Valley bakeries and California Special all-purpose flour for the retail market. The mill has continued to be a family run business with same location for 109 years and is managed by fourth and fifth generations as one of the few remaining independently owned flour mills left in the United States.

AROMAS

Whenever I pass a bakery, as I ride through a town,
I think of my mother's kitchen and fresh loaves, plump and rown.
I revel in scent of roses or the smell of new-mown hay;
A subtle perfume of lilacs can carry me far away.

But no scent made by Nature nor of the perfumer's art,
While they may give me pleasure, can really touch my heart.
Like that nostalgic fragrance that comes from new-maid bread,
It calls to life old memories that I had thought were dead.

Anna M. Priestley

METHODS AND PROCEDURES FOR PIES

CUTTING IN THE BUTTER

The GOLDEN FLAKE PIE DOUGH recipe in this chapter calls for half butter and half shortening. Be sure to use cold butter and only cut it into the flour until it resembles coarse meal. The shortening, which is softer, is cut in next. The shortening works into the flour faster, so by cutting in the cold butter first, the pie dough won't become overworked.

WORKING WITH THE DOUGH

After the liquids have been added to the flour mixture, work with the dough only enough to bind. Over-working the dough will make it tough. During the baking process, the tiny butter and shortening particles will melt, creating the desired flakiness in the crust.

ROLLING OUT THE DOUGH

Divide the dough in half, then shape each half into a smooth, flat ball. On a lightly floured board, roll one of the dough sections out round, by starting the rolling pin in the center of the dough and rolling if briefly back and forth. Rotate the dough, flouring the board slightly if necessary to keep it from sticking, and repeat the process in the opposite direction. Then, starting in the center again, roll the dough out to the perimeter where needed to create an even circle.

LINING THE PLATE OR FITTING THE PAN

After rolling out one section of the dough, fit it gently into the pie plate and allow the dough to fall into the corners to fit. If the dough is pushed or stretched, the sliced pie might not hold its shape when it is cut. Trim the pie dough 1 inch larger than the rim of the plate. If you are making a single-crust pie, such as lemon meringue, cream, nut, or any pie you would like to serve open-faced, turn the edge under and flute it. If you are making a double-crust or lattice pie, save the other half of the dough for the top, or, double the filling recipe and bake two pies, or, roll it out and fit it into another pie plate, flute the edges, prick with a fork, wrap it in plastic wrap and freeze it for another occasion.

BAKING THE CRUST BLIND

Line the pie plate or plates with the prepared crust, crimp the edges and prick the bottoms with a fork to vent out the steam so the bottoms will stay flat when baked. Pre-bake the crust in one of two ways.

STANDARD HOME METHOD

Most cream filled pies call for a pre-baked crust. In order for the crust to keep its shape during the baking process, most home bakers line the crust with waxed paper and then fill it with beans. They partially bake the crust, then remove the hot beans and paper after the sides are set and continue baking the crust until golden.

ADDING CUT-OUTS

Any leftover scraps of dough can be cut into decorative cut-outs. Place them on a parchment lined sheet pan, sprinkle with cinnamon-sugar if desired and bake them until golden, to be added later to the finished pie, adhering them with whipping cream. Or, they can be baked into the pie, such as a nut or fruit pie, or a double-crust pie. The cut-outs can be added right before the pie goes into the oven. On pumpkin or custard pies, pre-bake the pie for a short while before carefully adding the cut-outs.

HOLIDAY PIE

On the holidays, when from East and from West,
From North and from South come family and guest;
When the gray-haired American sees round his board
The old links of affection restored;
When the care–wearied man seeks his mother once more,
And the worn matron smiles where the girl smiled before;
What moistens the lip and what brightens the eye,
What calls back the past like holiday pie?

– Author Unknown

MOONS AND STARS BLACKBERRY PIE

YIELD: 1 PIE

GOLDEN FLAKE PIE CRUST

1 recipe, located on page 215.

FILLING

- 4 CUPS FRESH BLACKBERRIES
- 4 TABLESPOONS ALL-PURPOSE FLOUR
- 1 CUP SUGAR
- 2 TEASPOONS MINUTE TAPIOCA
- 4 TABLESPOONS (1 STICK) COLD BUTTER

COSMIC MILL

Perhaps the sky's a field of grain,
The Sun, a reaper rushing past;
Probably, after the summer rain,
Stars compose the wheat that's threshed.

Maybe the miller's the Man in the Moon
[Thunder would grind the starry wheat,
So on a snowy winter noon
Flour might tumble 'round our feet.]

- John Trimalchio

TO PREPARE THE CRUST

Prepare one recipe of GOLDEN FLAKE PIE DOUGH, following the instructions for a double-crust pie, as described on page 215.

TO PREPARE THE FILLING

Sort through the berries to remove any stems. Gently rinse them in a strainer under cold water to clean. Let drain.

Thoroughly mix together the flour, sugar and tapioca. Gently combine this mixture with the blackberries. Pour the berry mixture into the bottom pie crust. Cut the cold butter into small pieces and distribute it over the berry mixture.

On a lightly floured board, roll the top crust into a circle. Use moon and star cut-outs to make a pretty pattern in the center. Place the top crust on the pie, trim the excess, leaving a 1 inch rim. Gently roll the top crust under the bottom and flute the edge. Let stand 15 minutes.

TO BAKE

Preheat the oven to 350 degrees. Bake the pie in the fully preheated oven for 30 to 40 minutes, or until the top crust is golden and the insides just start to bubble. Cool to allow to thicken before slicing.

FIRST RHUBARB PIE

It's rosy as the sunset
In a quiet April sky,
Fragrant as hillside blossoms
When the wind is drifting by.
And always boys from eight to eighty
Feel their hearts beat high
The day they see and smell and taste
The first fresh rhubarb pie!

– Grace V. Watkins

STRAWBERRY RHUBARB PIE

GOLDEN FLAKE PIE CRUST

1 recipe, located on page 215.

FILLING

1¼ CUPS SUGAR

3 TABLESPOONS MINUTE TAPIOCA

¼ TEASPOON CINNAMON

¼ TEASPOON SALT

3 CUPS FRESH STRAWBERRIES, SLICED

2 CUPS RHUBARB, CUT INTO ½ INCH PIECES

1 TEASPOON GRATED ORANGE RIND

1 TABLESPOON BUTTER

OPTIONAL TOPPING

POWDERED SUGAR FOR DUSTING

TO PREPARE THE PIE CRUST

Prepare the GOLDEN FLAKE PIE DOUGH recipe located on page 215. Divide the dough in half. On a lightly floured board, roll one half of the dough into a circle. Gently fit the dough into the bottom of an 8 inch or 9 inch pie pan. Trim the edge, leaving a 1 inch overhang. Prick the bottom with a fork. Set the top crust aside.

TO PREPARE THE FILLING

In a large bowl, mix together the sugar, tapioca, cinnamon and salt. Add the sliced strawberries and cut up rhubarb and toss gently to coat. Let this mixture sit 10 minutes and then stir again. Pour the filling into the prepared bottom crust. Preheat the oven to 350 degrees.

TO PREPARE THE LATTICE TOP

Roll out the other half of the dough into a rectangle. Cut the dough into even stripes and weave them into a lattice pattern onto the top of the pie. Cut the edges of the strips, slightly larger than the bottom shell. Roll them under the bottom edge and flute into a pretty pattern.

TO BAKE

Bake in the fully preheated oven for 30-40 minutes, or until the lattice is golden and the insides are bubbling. Cool before slicing. Dust lightly with powdered sugar before serving.

PUMPKIN CREAM PIE

YIELD: 1 PIE

GOLDEN FLAKE PIE CRUST

1 recipe, located on page 215.

FILLING

3 CUPS PUMPKIN
¾ CUP SUGAR
½ TEASPOON SALT
½ TEASPOON NUTMEG
¼ TEASPOON CINNAMON
½ TEASPOON POWDERED GINGER
3 LARGE EGGS, LIGHTLY BEATEN
1 CUP HEAVY CREAM

GARNISH

2 CUPS WHIPPING CREAM
¼ CUP POWDERED SUGAR
1 TABLESPOON RUM FOR FLAVORING
¼ CUP CHOPPED PECANS

TO PREPARE THE PIE SHELL

Divide the dough in half. On a lightly floured board, roll each half to fit the bottom of two 8 inch or 9 inch pie tins. Flute the edges in a pretty pattern. Poke the bottoms of the crusts with a fork. Wrap one in plastic wrap and freeze for another use, or double the filling and make two pies.

Preheat the oven to 350 degrees.

TO PREPARE THE FILLING

Thoroughly mix together the pumpkin, sugar, salt, nutmeg, cinnamon and powdered ginger. Beat the eggs lightly and add them, along with the cream, and gently mix until well blended. Pour the filling into the prepared crust and bake in the preheated oven for 45 to 50 minutes, or until set. Cool.

TO SERVE

Whip the cream with the powdered sugar and rum until it holds soft peeks. Garnish each slice with a dollop and sprinkle with the chopped pecans.

POEM FOR A PUMPKIN PIE

Strange how a single pumkin pie can hold
So much of autumn in its flaky mold
There is the essence of the curving bin
And the stores of crib and cellar caught within
Its goodness, and the lovely carefree way,
Before the harvest, golden pumpkins lay
In near-by fields about the shocks of corn
Strange how within its fragrance there is borne
A sweet persisting thought of thankfullness,
And stranger still how one can repossess
Some childhood hour, and see in his mind's eye
His mother's kitchen, when eating pumpkin pie.

- Elaine V. Emans

GRANDMA'S CHERRY PIE

GOLDEN FLAKE PIE CRUST

1 recipe, located on page 215.

> 1 POUND FRESH CHERRIES, PITTED
> 1 CUP WATER
> 3 TABLESPOONS CORNSTARCH
> ¼ CUP PLUS 1 TABLESPOON SUGAR
> ¼ TEASPOON SALT
> 1 TEASPOON FINELY GRATED LEMON
> ¼ TEASPOON ALMOND EXTRACT

BOON TO PARENTS

Psychologically speaking, it's fortunate [very!]
That the tree G. Washington felled was a cherry
Instead of a maple or basswood or pine;
For parents attempting to mod and refine
Their own particular segment of youth
Can intersperse stories of George and the truth
With toothsome allusions to cherry pie
Or layer cake, scarlet and fruity and high;
While mention of cobbler or fresh cherry tarts
Will precipitate rapture in little dear's hearts.
Admittedly, lessons in ethics are relished
And longer remembered when pastry embellished.

– Grace V. Watkins

TO PREPARE THE FILLING

Wash, stem and pit the fresh cherries. In a large saucepan, whisk together the water, cornstarch, sugar, salt and grated lemon peel. Add the cherries and bring this mixture to a full boil, whisking often. Cool the filling while you prepare the pie crust. Preheat the oven to 350 degrees.

TO PREPARE THE PIE SHELL

Divide the dough in half. On a lightly floured board, roll one half to fit the bottom of an 8 inch or 9 inch pie tin. Prick the bottom with a fork. After the filling has cooled, pour it into the prepared shell. Roll out the top crust and top the pie. Turn the top crust under the bottom and flute the edges together. Cut several vents in the top of the pie.

TO BAKE

Bake the pie in the fully preheated oven for 30-40 minutes or until the filling starts to bubble and the crust is golden. Cool before slicing.

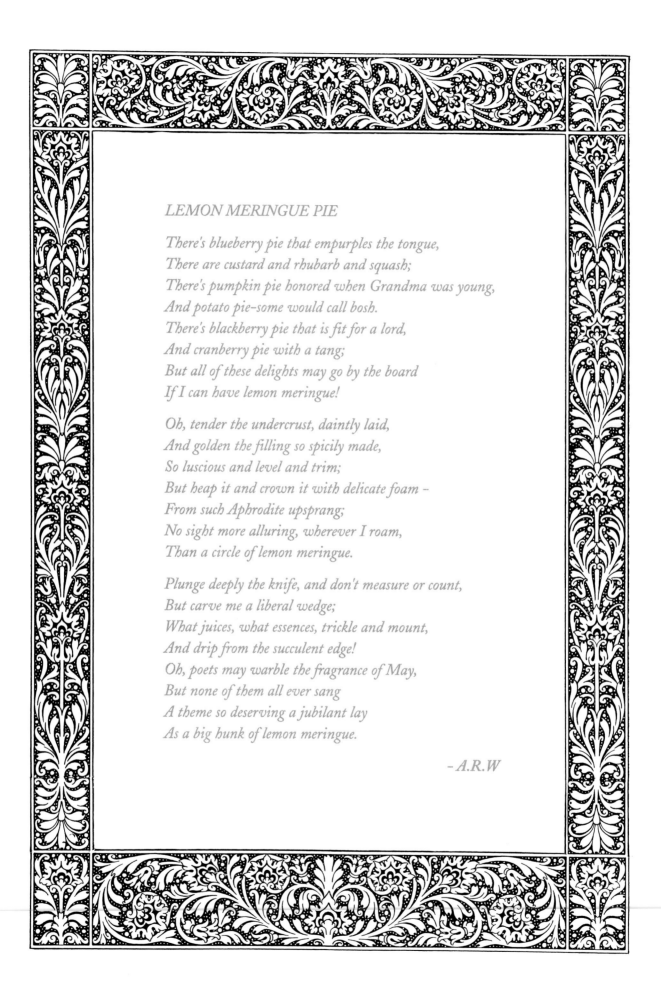

LEMON MERINGUE PIE

There's blueberry pie that empurples the tongue,
There are custard and rhubarb and squash;
There's pumpkin pie honored when Grandma was young,
And potato pie–some would call bosh.
There's blackberry pie that is fit for a lord,
And cranberry pie with a tang;
But all of these delights may go by the board
If I can have lemon meringue!

Oh, tender the undercrust, daintly laid,
And golden the filling so spicily made,
So luscious and level and trim;
But heap it and crown it with delicate foam –
From such Aphrodite upsprang;
No sight more alluring, wherever I roam,
Than a circle of lemon meringue.

Plunge deeply the knife, and don't measure or count,
But carve me a liberal wedge;
What juices, what essences, trickle and mount,
And drip from the succulent edge!
Oh, poets may warble the fragrance of May,
But none of them all ever sang
A theme so deserving a jubilant lay
As a big hunk of lemon meringue.

– A.R.W

ETHEREAL LEMON MERINGUE PIE

GOLDEN FLAKE PIE CRUST

1 recipe, located on page 215.

FILLING

> 7 TABLESPOONS CORNSTARCH
> 1½ CUPS SUGAR
> ¼ TEASPOON SALT
> 1½ CUPS HOT WATER
> 3 EGG YOLKS
> 1 TEASPOON FRESH LEMON ZEST
> ½ CUP FRESH LEMON JUICE
> 2 TABLESPOONS BUTTER

MERINGUE TOPPING

> 9 EGG WHITES
> 1 CUP PLUS 2 TABLESPOONS SUGAR
> 1 TABLESPOON FRESH LEMON JUICE

TO PREPARE THE PIE SHELL

Divide the dough in half. On a lightly floured board, roll each half to fit the bottom of two 8 inch or 9 inch pie tins. Flute the edges in a pretty pattern. Poke the bottoms of the crusts with a fork. Wrap one in plastic wrap and freeze for another use. Bake the shell blind as described on page 195. Cool.

TO PREPARE THE FILLING

In a large saucepan, mix together until thoroughly blended the cornstarch, sugar and salt. Add the hot water and beat with the whisk until smooth. In a small bowl, beat the egg yolks. Pour approximately ¼ of the cornstarch mixture into the egg yolks and beat again.

On medium heat, bring the remaining cornstarch mixture to a boil, continually beating with a whisk. Beat in the yolk mixture and continue beating, cooking the mixture until it comes to a full boil and is thick. Remove the filling from the heat and stir in the fresh lemon zest, fresh lemon juice and the butter. Stir until smooth. Allow to cool for 15 minutes. Pour the filling into the pre-baked, cooled crust. Place it into the refrigerator and allow to cool completely while you prepare the topping.

TO PREPARE THE MERINGUE TOPPING

After the pie has cooled, beat the egg whites on medium speed with an electric mixer. Continue beating, adding the sugar, one tablespoon at a time. Add the 1 tablespoon of fresh lemon juice and continue beating until the whites are stiff but not dry. Using a pastry bag fitted with a pastry tip, pipe the meringue onto the pie in a pretty pattern, or pile the meringue onto the pie with a large spoon.

TO BAKE

Preheat the oven to 350 degrees. Place the topped pie into the oven for 5 to 10 minutes, or until the meringue is golden. Watch it carefully and turn it if necessary to brown evenly. Cool for 1 hour at room temperature, then chill in the refrigerator until serving time.

SUBLIME LIME CREAM PIE

GOLDEN FLAKE PIE CRUST

1 recipe, located on page 215.

PIE FILLING

1⅓ CUPS SUGAR

4 TABLESPOONS CORNSTARCH

6 TABLESPOONS BUTTER, CUT INTO PIECES

1½ TABLESPOONS FINELY GRATED LIME RIND

½ CUP FRESH LIME JUICE

1⅓ CUPS LIGHT CREAM

PIE TOPPING

1 CUP WHIPPING CREAM

¼ CUP POWDERED SUGAR

3 TABLESPOONS SOUR CREAM

FINELY GRATED LIME RIND

NEIGHBOR - OLD STYLE

Great-aunt Carrie loved to take
Pies and cookies, biscuits, cake
And other good things she would bake
Out to her neighbors, sick or well,
Then she'd sit and "rest a spell"
And hear the news they had to tell.

Her pleasure was so innocent,
Her visits always so well-meant
She found a welcome wherever she went.
Now folks recall her basket, high
With devil's food and lemon pie,
And wish her back...and so do I.

- Eloise Wade Hackett

TO PREPARE THE PIE SHELL

Divide the dough in half. On a lightly floured board, roll each half to fit the bottom of two 8 inch or 9 inch pie tins. Flute the edges in a pretty pattern. Poke the bottoms of the crusts with a fork. Wrap one in plastic wrap and freeze for another use. Bake the other shell blind as described on page 195. Cool.

TO PREPARE THE FILLING

In a medium size saucepan, whisk together the sugar and cornstarch until well blended. Add the butter, the finely grated lime rind, fresh lime juice and light cream. Heat, stirring until the butter melts. Cook, continually stirring until the mixture comes to a full boil. Remove from the heat and let cool. Pour into the prepared, cooled crust and chill for 4 hours or until set.

TO PREPARE THE TOPPING

Whip the cream and powdered sugar together until stiff. Blend in the sour cream. Pipe from a pastry bag, using a large star pastry tip, the topping onto the chilled pie in a pretty pattern. Sprinkle with the finely grated lime rind.

CRUMB TOPPED FRENCH APPLE PIE

YIELD: 1 PIE

GOLDEN FLAKE PIE CRUST

1 recipe, located on page 213.

FILLING

¼ CUP ALL-PURPOSE FLOUR
1 TO 1½ CUPS SUGAR
½ TEASPOON CINNAMON
⅛ TEASPOON NUTMEG
⅛ TEASPOON SALT
8 CUPS SLICED PEELED APPLES
1 TABLESPOON LEMON JUICE
2 TABLESPOONS BUTTER

CRUMB TOPPING

½ CUP (1 STICK) COLD BUTTER
½ CUP ALL-PURPOSE FLOUR
½ CUP BROWN SUGAR
1 TEASPOON CINNAMON
¼ CUP CHOPPED WALNUTS

APPLE PIES BAKING

The scent of apple blossom we loved well
Was only a prelude to this richer smell
Of fruit now ruddy, glowing in the grass.
And the remembrance of Spring airs will pass
Away still further before the breath-taking
Fragrance, directly, of apple pies baking!

- Elaine V. Emans

TO PREPARE THE PIE SHELL

Prepare one recipe of GOLDEN FLAKE PIE DOUGH. Divide the dough in half. On a lightly floured board, roll each half to fit the bottom of two 8 inch or 9 inch pie tins. Flute the edges in a pretty pattern. Poke the bottoms of the crusts with a fork. Wrap one in plastic wrap and freeze for another use, or double the filling and make two pies. Do not pre-bake.

TO PREPARE THE FILLING

Combine the flour and the sugar in a large bowl. The amount of sugar depends on the tartness of the apples. Mix in the cinnamon, nutmeg and salt. Toss in the apples and lemon juice to coat. Pile into the prepared crust. Dot with the butter.

TO PREPARE THE CRUMB TOPPING

Cut the cold butter into small pieces and place into a food processor. Add the flour, brown sugar and the cinnamon. Process briefly until the mixture resembles coarse meal. Add the chopped walnuts and process briefly again. Pile evenly onto the pie and bake in a fully preheated 350 degree oven for 40-50 minutes or until the apples feel tender when tested by inserting a paring knife.

KITCHEN MAGIC

There's magic in my kitchen
That makes the biscuits rise,
That puts the jell in jellies
And the flakiness in pies.

There's a magic in the sparkle
Of my man's approving eyes
As he views with pride the baking
And the baker of those pies!

– Rigmor Stone

OLD FASHIONED CHESS PIE

GOLDEN FLAKE PIE CRUST

1 recipe, located on page 215.

FILLING

½ CUP BUTTER (1 STICK)
1½ CUPS SUGAR
3 EGGS
5 TABLESPOONS MILK
1½ CUPS RAISINS
1½ CUPS CHOPPED WALNUTS
1½ TEASPOONS VANILLA

TOPPING

UNSWEETENED WHIPPED CREAM

Preheat the oven to 350 degrees.

TO PREPARE THE PIE SHELL

Prepare one recipe of GOLDEN FLAKE PIE DOUGH. Divide the dough in half. On a lightly floured board, roll each half to fit the bottom of two 8 inch or 9 inch pie tins. Flute the edges in a pretty pattern. Poke the bottoms of the crusts with a fork. Wrap one in plastic wrap and freeze for another use, or double the filling and make two pies. Do not pre-bake.

FOR THE FILLING

Cream together the butter and sugar. Beat in the eggs and milk. Add the raisins, walnuts and vanilla and mix well.

Spread the filling into the prepared crust. Bake in the fully preheated oven for 35 to 45 minutes or until the crust is golden and the top of the pie is a rich brown, slightly firm to the touch. Cool to warm before serving. Serve with dollops of unsweetened whipped cream.

ENCHANTING STRAWBERRY CHEESE PIE

GOLDEN FLAKE PIE CRUST

1 recipe, located on page 213.

FILLING

12 OUNCES CREAM CHEESE
½ CUP SUGAR
1½ TEASPOONS FINELY GRATED ORANGE RIND
3 TABLESPOONS FRESH ORANGE JUICE
3 TABLESPOONS LIGHT CREAM
1 EGG

TOPPING

4 CUPS FRESH STRAWBERRIES
2 CUPS SUGAR
5 TABLESPOONS CORNSTARCH
2 TABLESPOONS FRESH LEMON JUICE

TO PREPARE THE PIE SHELL

Divide the dough in half and line two 9 inch pie pans. Flute the edges and prick the bottoms with a fork. Wrap one in plastic wrap and freeze to use at another time. Bake the other blind, as described on page 195 in a fully preheated 350 degree oven, only long enough to set the sides, about 10 minutes. Turn the shell right side up and carefully remove the top pie plate.

TO PREPARE THE FILLING

Beat the cream cheese with the ½ cup sugar until smooth. Add the grated orange rind, orange juice and light cream. Add the egg and beat on low until well incorporated. Pour this mixture into the prepared, partially baked shell and bake for 20 minutes or until the filling feels set when touched lightly in the center. Cool.

TO PREPARE THE TOPPING

Sort the berries according to size and save the most uniform ones for the top. Mix the other half in a food processor for a brief moment or mash them well with a potato masher. Place the mashed berries into a saucepan.

In a small bowl, mix together the 2 cups sugar and the cornstarch until smooth. Add this mixture to the berries along with the fresh lemon juice. Cook over medium heat, stirring constantly, until the mixture comes to a full boil and thickens. Cool. Pour the cooled topping onto the cooled pie. Arrange the remaining berries, (cut-side-down) onto the pie. Chill until set.

RECOLLECTION IN AUGUST

Aunt Mary's hands were soft and white;
There was a faint perfume
From yellow marigolds she wore
When summer was in bloom.

Aunt Martha's hands were hard and brown,
She wore no flower bouquet.
But oh the sweet crust she could make,
Gold as an August day!

And often in a summer noon
I long to taste again
The berry pie Aunt Martha made
Once for a lad of ten!

– Grace V. Watkins

MACADAMIA NUT PIE

Prepare one recipe of GOLDEN FLAKE PIE DOUGH, located on the next page. Follow the instructions for an open faced pie, line an 8 inch pie plate.

FILLING

3 EGGS

1 CUP LIGHT CORN SYRUP

⅔ CUP SUGAR

2 TABLESPOONS MELTED BUTTER

1 TEASPOON VANILLA

1½ CUPS COARSELY CHOPPED, MACADAMIA NUTS

LIGHTLY SWEETENED WHIPPED CREAM

Whose golden crust I eat, her song I sing.

- German saying.

Beat together thoroughly the eggs, light corn syrup, sugar, melted butter and the vanilla. Mix in the chopped nuts. Pour the filling into the prepared crust and bake for 45 to 50 minutes or until the top is golden and the filling is set. Cool. Serve with dollops whipped cream.

GOLDEN FLAKE PIE CRUST

PIE CRUST

3 CUPS ALL-PURPOSE FLOUR
½ TEASPOON SALT
5 OUNCES COLD BUTTER, CUT UP
5 OUNCES SHORTENING
1 EGG
6 TABLESPOONS COLD WATER
1 TABLESPOON WHITE VINEGAR

LOVES LABOR

"How much I baked with ten around the table
For years and years," she said,"I hate to guess.
My rhubarb pies would cover half an acre,
And loaves of bread! The number's limitless.
Square rods of Devil's Food, and miles of cookies,
And wheat cakes that would stack up mountain-high.
I loved it and I don't like being idle.
If no one minds I'll go and bake a pie,"

- Eloise Wade Hackett

TO PREPARE THE DOUGH

Place the flour and salt into a medium size mixing bowl. On medium speed, or with a pastry cutter, cut the cold butter into the flour until the mixture resembles course meal, then cut in the shortening.

In a small bowl, beat together the egg, cold water and vinegar. Add approximately ½ cup of the flour mixture to the wet ingredients and mix with a fork to blend. Pour this mixture into the flour bowl , and mix on low speed just until the dough starts to leave the sides of the bowl, or toss with a fork or your fingers to bind.

DOUBLE CRUST PIE

Divide the dough in half. On a lightly floured board, roll one half of the dough into a circle. Gently fit the dough into the bottom of an 8 inch or 9 inch pie pan. Trim the edge, leaving a ¾ inch overhang. Prick the bottom several times with a fork. Prepare the filling and fill the pie shell.

On a clean, lightly floured board, roll the top crust into a circle. Use decorative cutouts to create a vented pattern in the top. Carefully place the top, evenly centered on the pie. Trim the edges even with the bottom crust. Gently press the edges together and roll them under. Flute or crimp the edges into a pretty, uniform pattern.

OPEN FACED PIE

Divide the prepared dough in half. Roll out each portion the fit an 8 inch or 9 inch pie plate. Gently fit the dough into the pans, leaving a 1 inch overhang. Turn the edges under and crimp. Prick the bottoms and sides with a fork. Wrap one in plastic wrap and freeze for another occasion, or double the filling and make two pies.

BAKING BLIND

Follow the directions in the PROPER BAKING PROCEDURES FOR PIES, page 195.

CONTENTMENT

The ever moving water
Passing swiftly through the race;
The crunching, crunching
Of the stones set face to face;
The miller busy grinding,
Singing, whistling, always finding
Music in the rumble,
With a smile upon his face.
For in contentment there is glory
[And for glory some men die],
But the gentle, happy miller
Has more joy than you and I.

- Ralph Scallon Herman

CHAPTER SEVEN

DELECTABLE CAKES

DEDICATED TO THE SHAWNEE MILLING COMPANY

EST. 1891

SHAWNEE MILLING COMPANY

The original Shawnee flour mill was built in the Tecumseh, Oklahoma Indian Territory in 1891 by a Mr. Woodward (with the help of Jess Johnson and his sister), who was employed by the Jones Milling Company. The mill, built with large wooden timbers, furnished flour and corn meal to the early white settlers and to several Indian tribes, comprised of the Shawnees, the Pottawatomies, the Sac and Fox, the Kickapoos, the Seminoles, the Choctaws and others.

In 1895, the town of Shawnee was founded, and with the coming of the Choctaw-Oklahoma and Gulf Railroad in 1896 (later to become the Chicago, Rock Island and Pacific Railway) and later the Santa Fe in 1902, the foundation was laid for the development of a growing city. The town of Shawnee donated a new site in 1897 and the roller mill was pulled across the river with mules to its present location in Shawnee. It was operated by the families of Catlin and Carey under the name of Shawnee Roller Mills.

On April 24th, 1906, the mill was purchased from Mrs. Catlin by a flour salesman, Mr. John Lloyd Ford, and the name was changed from Shawnee Roller Mills to Shawnee Milling Company. At that time, the wooden mill had a daily capacity of 150 cwts. and 15,000 bushels of grain storage.

Over time, the mill capacity was increased and six other small mills were acquired by Ford, five in Oklahoma and one in Kansas. The most important was in Okeene, purchased in 1917.

Today the Shawnee Milling Company is the largest Oklahoma-owned milling company. For the past ninety years the company has been successfully run by the Ford family, now in their third generation. The company employs over 200 people, serves both the family and bakery trade, and manufactures hundreds of products which it sells to 35 states. The Shawnee Milling company will celebrate its Centennial in the year 2006.

NATURE'S MILLER DUSTING

Ho, Nature's miller dusting,
Throughout the hours of night,
With steady hand encrusting
He robes the earth in white.

And all his finer sifting
So powdery, so light,
The rude March wind is drifting
To pile it left and right.

He dusts upon the bridges,
On every field and hedge,
The rugged mountain ridges,
Each porch and window ledge.

And when his task is finished,
The miller hides away
With skill all undiminished
To dust another day.

Alas, this pure adorning
Beneath the miller's sway,
For Sol's swift brush at morning
May sweep it all away.

- Nellie Lawrence

PROPER BAKING PROCEDURES FOR CAKES

PREHEATING THE OVEN

Start preheating the oven before you make the cake batter so that the cake can go into the oven right away. This way the leavening agents used will not loose their strength.

MIXING THE BATTER

Cream the butter and sugar together thoroughly before adding the other ingredients or you may end up with holes in your cake. Add the eggs, or any liquid, slowly. Throughout the mixing process, be sure to scrape the sides and bottom of the bowl often to ensure a uniform batter. Be sure not to over-mix the batter, and be sure to divide it evenly between the pans so that it will uniformly bake.

CHECKING FOR DONENESS

The cake is done if it springs back when touched lightly in the center.

MAKING A CAKE BOARD

If you don't have a serving plate large enough, you can make a cake board by covering a square piece of heavy cardboard, slightly larger than the circumference of the cake with white butcher paper, taping it securely underneath. Center white doilies on the top, then cover with plastic wrap, taping it firmly to the bottom. To shrink-wrap the board, preheat the oven and carefully balance the board on your hand, then hold it in the oven for a few seconds and the plastic will shrink slightly and tighten.

If you are taking a special dessert to a dinner party or a birthday gathering, one of the many advantages of making a cake board is that you don't have to worry about retrieving it after the party is over. The birthday honoree can keep any leftover cake and the hostess always appreciates its simplicity.

BAKING LARGER QUANTITIES / MAKING A CAKE FRAME

Depending on the size of your oven, cut 4 inch wide strips of cardboard slightly larger than the width and length of your half-sheet or full-sheet pan. Fold the corners to fit and tape the ends together, making a frame that fits exactly into the pan. Line the frame with parchment paper, folding it in the corners so that the cake batter can't leak out. Carefully pour the batter into the frame and increase the baking time.

WHEN MARIE MAKES ANGEL FOOD

When sister Marie makes angel food
No other cake can vie with hers.
Angelic is our every mood
When this divine event occurs.

Even our cat, old Gadsie, purrs
With satisfaction when his glance
Includes the magic spoon that stirs
Such dreams as cause our hearts to dance.

When sister Marie makes angel food
ll little kiddies "off the beam"
Become a sweet, seraphic brood,
With sprouting wings and souls that gleam.

- Robert Cary

HEART POUND CAKE

CAKE BATTER

- 2 CUPS WHITE, ALL-PURPOSE FLOUR
- 2 TEASPOONS BAKING POWDER
- ¼ TEASPOON SALT
- 12 TABLESPOONS (1½ STICKS) BUTTER
- ¾ CUP SUGAR
- 3 EGGS
- 1 TEASPOON VANILLA
- ½ CUP MILK
- 1 TO 2 TEASPOONS FRESH LEMON ZEST

SMALL BOY IN VARIETY STORE

He turns up his nose at the paper lace
That edges a crimson valentine,
And a withering scorn spreads over his face
At the verse with sentimental line.
But suddenly scorn gives way to rapture
That glitters and gleams within his eyes
As he reaches his eager hand to capture
The fair and irresistible prize –
A heart-shaped cake of red and white,
With ecstasy promised in every bite!

- Grace V. Watkins

LEMON CURD

1 recipe lemon curd, found on page 177 (optional accompaniment).

Preheat the oven to 350 degrees.

TO PREPARE THE PAN

Lightly grease the sides of a heart shaped cake pan and line the bottom with parchment paper to fit, or lightly grease a 9 inch by 5 inch loaf pan.

TO PREPARE THE BATTER

Sift together the flour, baking powder and salt and set aside. In a large mixing bowl, thoroughly cream the butter and sugar. Add the eggs, one at a time, scraping the bottom of the bowl after each addition. Add the vanilla.

Add half the dry ingredients to the butter mixture and mix until smooth. Add half of the milk and mix again. Add the other half of the dry ingredients to the batter, then add the remaining milk and the fresh lemon zest. Mix again briefly until smooth. Pour the batter into the prepared pan.

TO BAKE

Bake the pound cake in the fully preheated oven for 40-50 minutes, or until a toothpick inserted in the center comes out clean. Serve warm, or at room temperature with a dollop of fresh lemon curd if so desired.

HER FIRST CAKE

Proudly she dons her apron,
Gaily she gets the eggs,
Carefully sifts the flour,
Restlessly shifts plump legs;

Breathlessly whirls the beater,
fills up the sugar cup,
Spills a bit of the flavoring,
Beats the gold batter up:

Pours it with fingers shaking,
Smiles at me hovering near,
Shoots it in oven all heated –
"Call when it's done, darling dear!"

– Author unknown

TO-PINE-FOR PINEAPPLE CAKE

CAKE

2 CUPS ALL-PURPOSE FLOUR

1¼ CUPS SUGAR

2 TABLESPOONS BAKING SODA

1 (20 OUNCE) CAN CRUSHED PINEAPPLE WITH JUICE

2 EGGS

½ CUP VEGETABLE OIL

TOPPING

½ CUP BUTTER

1¼ CUPS SUGAR

1 (5.33 OUNCE) CAN EVAPORATED MILK

1 CUP SHREDDED COCONUT

½ TEASPOON VANILLA

1 CUP CHOPPED WALNUTS

Preheat the oven to 350 degrees.

TO PREPARE THE PAN

Lightly butter a 9 inch by 13 inch pan.

TO PREPARE THE CAKE

Sift the flour, sugar and baking soda into a large bowl. In another bowl, whisk together the crushed pineapple with its juice, eggs and oil. Pour the wet ingredients into the dry and mix until moistened. Pour the batter into the prepared pan.

TO BAKE

Bake the cake in the fully preheated oven for 30 minutes, or until a toothpick inserted in the center comes out clean. Prepare the topping while the cake is baking.

TO PREPARE THE TOPPING

In a large saucepan over medium heat, bring to a boil the butter, sugar and evaporated milk. Boil, without stirring, for 3 to 4 minutes. Remove from the heat, cool slightly, then stir in the coconut, vanilla and chopped walnuts. Remove the cake from the oven when it is through baking and immediately spread the hot topping on the cake. Serve warm or at room temperature.

ALMOND AMARETTO TORTÉ

PASTRY

    1⅓ CUPS ALL-PURPOSE FLOUR
    1 TEASPOON BAKING POWDER
    ⅓ CUP SUGAR
    ½ TEASPOON SALT
    ½ CUP BUTTER, AT ROOM TEMPERATURE
    1 EGG YOLK

FILLING

    1 CUP BUTTER
    1⅓ CUPS SUGAR
    2⅔ CUPS FINELY GROUND BLANCHED ALMONDS
    1 TEASPOON ALMOND EXTRACT
    3 TABLESPOONS GRAND MARNIER OR AMARETTO
    2 EGGS
    2 EGG YOLKS
    POWDERED SUGAR FOR DUSTING

Preheat the oven to 350 degrees.

SUMMER OWNS A COTTAGE

Summer owns a cottage;
It is thatched with leaves.
Roses planted by the door
Camber to the eaves.
Her raftered, roomy kitchen,
Neat as any pin;
A sunshine cake cools on a shelf
In a shiny tin.
Sitting at a window,
The lattice open wide,
She hums while her canary sings –
A checkered apron tied
About her ample waist – and as
She slowly rocks, she sews
Strips of rags to roll in balls:
Here's every green that grows –
Wheat and corn and apple-green,
Alfalfa, oats and rye –
Oh, what a carpet she will weave
For her parlor, by – and – by!

- Ethel Romig Fuller

TO PREPARE THE CRUST

Sift together the flour, baking powder, sugar and salt. Add the butter and egg yolk and mix well until the dough forms a smooth ball. Place the dough between two sheets of waxed paper and roll it out in a circle 1½ inches larger then the bottom of a 12 inch, removeable bottom pan. Refrigerate the dough until it is cold. Press the dough into the bottom and up the sides of the tart pan.

TO PREPARE THE FILLING

Cream together the butter and sugar. Add the ground almonds, the almond extract and the liqueur. Beat in the eggs and the egg yolks. Pour the filling into the prepared crust.

TO BAKE

Place a baking sheet on the lower rack of your oven to catch any butter that seeps out of the torte as it bakes. Bake in the fully preheated oven for 40-50 minutes, or until the sides of the torte are golden brown and it starts to puff up slightly. Cool to warm before removing from the pan. Cool completely before dusting with powdered sugar.

GLUNKY CARROT CAKE

CAKE BATTER

3 CUPS ALL-PURPOSE FLOUR

1½ TEASPOONS BAKING SODA

1 TEASPOON CINNAMON

½ TEASPOON SALT

1½ CUPS OIL

2 CUPS SUGAR

2 CUPS GRATED, RAW CARROTS

1 CAN (8½ OUNCES)
  CRUSHED PINEAPPLE WITH JUICE

1 CUP CHOPPED WALNUTS

1 CUP RAISINS

¾ CUP COCONUT

2 TEASPOONS VANILLA

3 EGGS

ICING

2 POUNDS CREAM CHEESE,
  FAIRLY SOFT

1 POUND BUTTER, FAIRLY SOFT

2 TO 3 (1 POUND) BOXES
  POWDERED SUGAR

1 TABLESPOON VANILLA

1 CUP CHOPPED WALNUTS
  OR PECANS (OPTIONAL)

1 CUP RAISINS (OPTIONAL)

Ovens containing cakes and breads were unearthed when Pompeii was uncovered, after having been buried by the ashes and lava of the Vesuvius volcano for more than 1900 years.

- The Northwestern Miller

TO PREPARE THE PANS

Place two 9" or 10" round pans, preferably with removable bottoms, on a sheet of parchment paper. Trace a circle around them and cut the circle to fit the pan. Lightly grease the sides.

TO PREPARE THE CAKE

Sift together the flour, baking soda, cinnamon and salt. Beat together the oil, sugar, grated carrots, pineapple with juice, chopped walnuts, raisins, coconut and vanilla and mix well. Add the dry ingredients to the wet, beating only enough to moisten. Add the eggs until well blended. Pour the batter into the prepared pans.

TO BAKE

Bake the cake in the fully preheated 350 degree oven for 30 minutes to 1 hour, depending on the size of your pans, until the center feels firm to the touch. Cool completely before frosting.

TO PREPARE THE ICING

Cream together the cream cheese and the butter. Sift in the powdered sugar, one cup at a time and beat until smooth. Add the vanilla. Measure out about ⅓ of the frosting and set aside. Add the chopped walnuts and raisins to the other ⅔ rds and mix only enough to blend. Frost the cooled cake between the two layers and around the outside and top with the frosting to which you have added the nuts and raisins. Use the remaining icing to pipe a pretty pattern around the top, reserving a small portion, if desired, for decorating the cake with carrots, or a special greeting.

If desired, lightly press chopped walnuts or pecans into the sides.

COZY CARROT SPICE CAKE

CAKE BATTER

1½ CUPS GRATED, RAW CARROTS

1⅓ CUPS WATER

1⅓ CUPS BROWN SUGAR

1 CUP GOLDEN RAISINS

¼ CUP BUTTER

1 TEASPOON CLOVES

1 TEASPOON CINNAMON

1 TEASPOON NUTMEG

2 CUPS ALL-PURPOSE FLOUR

½ TEASPOON SODA

1 TEASPOON BAKING POWDER

¼ TEASPOON SALT

ICING

1 CUP BUTTER

1 (1 POUND) BOX POWDERED SUGAR

1 TEASPOON VANILLA

1 EGG YOLK

TO PREPARE THE CAKE

In a large pan, combine the grated carrots, water, brown sugar, golden raisins, butter, cloves, cinnamon and nutmeg. Bring this mixture to a boil, reduce the heat and simmer gently for 5 minutes. Remove from the heat and cool to room temperature.

Preheat the oven to 350 degrees. Butter a 9 inch by 13 inch pan, or several small loaf pans.

Sift together the flour, baking soda, baking powder and salt. After the hot mixture has cooled to room temperature, mix the wet ingredients with the dry, only enough to thoroughly blend. Pour the batter into the prepared pan or pans.

TO BAKE

Bake in the fully preheated oven until the center feels firm to the touch. Cool completely before slicing.

TO PREPARE THE ICING

Beat the butter with the powdered sugar until creamy. Add the vanilla and the egg yolk and beat until smooth. Frost the cooled cake or loaves. Wrap the loaves with ribbons and holly leaves if desired.

THOUGHTS WHILE MAKING A SPICE CAKE

I measure cloves and dream of Zanzibar,
I dip my spoon in cinnamon and know
It may have come to me from Borneo,
I add the nutmeg, wondering if far
Sumatra furnished me with such a flavor –
And when I return the spices to their shelf,
I think how each is perfect in itself.
But presently the cake will rise, and savor
Of such a wedding of aromas through
The house that I shall wonder what device
Of culinary art caught up the spice –
And, when you come for lunch and taste it,
You will praise it so I will not question weather
Much magic lies in spices mixed together!

– Elaine V. Emans

BIRTHDAY CAKE

On my sister's birthday, when she was ten,
Our Aunt Miranda arrived, and then
Announced she would make the party cake.
I watched her mix the batter and take
A thimble, a dime and a little ring
And drop them in, that morning in spring.
"Old maid, rich husband, and earliest wed,"
She said.
It's as well Aunt Miranda never knew
That the little girl with eyes of blue,
The one who got the slice with the thimble,
Has been three times matrimonially nimble,

The dime girl's husband is as poor as a mouse,
And the one with the ring's still missing a spouse!
Oh, well, the sugary cake was heaven
To a younger brother of seven!

– Grace V. Watkins

INTENSE CHOCOLATE ORANGE TRUFFLE TORTÉ

TORTE BATTER

14 OUNCES, FINELY CHOPPED, SEMI-SWEET GUITTARD CHOCOLATE

12 TABLESPOONS (1½ STICKS) BUTTER

8 EGG YOLKS

8 EGG WHITES

6 TABLESPOONS SUGAR, DIVIDED

GRATED ZEST OF ONE ORANGE

4 TABLESPOONS ALL-PURPOSE FLOUR

PINCH OF SALT

TORTE FILLING

12 OUNCES, FINELY CHOPPED, SEMI-SWEET GUITTARD CHOCOLATE

4 TABLESPOONS (½ STICK) BUTTER

1 TABLESPOON INSTANT ESPRESSO POWDER

2 TABLESPOONS COLD BUTTER

⅔ CUP WHIPPING CREAM

2 TABLESPOONS SOUR CREAM

TORTE ICING

½ CUP PLUS 2 TABLESPOONS HEAVY CREAM

3 TABLESPOONS BUTTER

10 OUNCES, FINELY CHOPPED, SEMI-SWEET GUITTARD CHOCOLATE

1½ TABLESPOONS COLD BUTTER

TO PREPARE THE PANS

Place two 10 inch pans (preferably with removable bottoms) on a piece of parchment paper and trace a circle around them. Cut the circles and fit them into the pans. Butter the sides and dust lightly with flour.

TO PREPARE THE TORTE BATTER

Melt the chocolate and butter together over very low heat. Cool to lightly warm. Beat the egg yolks with 3 tablespoons of the sugar until they are a light lemon color. Fold the beaten egg yolks into the melted chocolate and butter mixture. In a separate clean bowl, beat the egg whites with the other 3 tablespoons of sugar until stiff but not dry. Sift the flour over the egg whites and fold it in. Carefully fold the chocolate mixture into the beaten egg white mixture. Divide the batter evenly between the two prepared pans.

TO BAKE

Bake in a fully preheated oven (350 degrees) until the torte's middle is firm to the touch. Cool the torte completely before adding the filling.

TO PREPARE THE FILLING AND ASSEMBLE

Gently heat the chopped chocolate and butter together, stirring it with a spatula until smooth. Remove from the heat and stir in the espresso powder and the cold butter. Allow to cool to warm. Whip the cream until stiff, then mix in the sour cream. Fold it into the cooled, melted chocolate mixture.

After the cakes have cooled completely, turn them upside down and remove them from the pans, then carefully remove the parchment paper. Using a sharp, serrated knife, slice them in half. You will then have four layers.

In a clean pan, the same size as the one the cakes were baked in, line the bottom with a circle of parchment paper. (This step is not necessary if your pan has a removable bottom). Next line the pan with one of the cake layers. Pour ¼ of the filling onto the layer and spread it evenly to cover. Place another cake layer on the top spread with another ¼ of the filling. Repeat this process 2 more times, ending with filling on top. Put the pan between your hands and gently shake it to get the filling to fill up the sides. Place the torte in the refrigerator overnight or until set.

TO PREPARE THE TOPPING

Heat the cream with the butter in a small pan until melted. Remove from the heat and stir in the chopped chocolate until smooth. Add the cold butter and stir until smooth. Chill the topping if necessary, stirring from time to time, until it is spreadable.

TO ASSEMBLE THE TORTE

Gently run a sharp knife around the inside edge of the well-chilled pan. Carefully slide the removable bottom up to remove the cake. Run a knife under the bottom of the cake and slide it onto a cooling rack which is sitting on parchment paper. When the topping is ready, using a pastry knife, spread it evenly around the sides of the cake. After the sides are smooth, spread the remainder on the top. Wait for the topping to set slightly, then make a pattern in the top by running your knife back and forth (once or twice), creating an even wave pattern. Chill the cake thoroughly, then carefully run a knife around the bottom edge of the cake to give it a clean edge and carefully lift and slide it onto a cake plate to serve.

NOTE

This topping is wonderful to work with because if it gets too cold, you can warm it slightly. If it gets too warm you can chill it slightly until you have the right consistency.

MOM'S FAITHFUL CHOCOLATE CAKE

CAKE BATTER

- 2 CUPS BOILING WATER
- 1 CUP COCOA, SUCH AS HERSHEYS
- 1 CUP BUTTER (2 STICKS)
- 2½ CUPS SUGAR
- 1½ TEASPOONS VANILLA
- 2¾ CUPS ALL PURPOSE FLOUR
- 2 TEASPOONS BAKING SODA
- ½ TEASPOON BAKING POWDER
- ½ TEASPOON SALT
- 4 EGGS, SLIGHTLY BEATEN

Preheat the oven to 350 degrees.

LICKIN' GOOD

When Grandma had a baking day
We children would enroll
As kitchen helpers so we'd be
On hand to lick the bowl.

We couldn't wait for cakes to bake:
We sought a nearer goal
And scamper off when we'd licked clean
The beater, spoon and bowl.

The pattern is repeated now
For children still cajole
Their Grandma [me] to have a chance
To lick the mixing bowl.

– Eloise Wade Hackett

TO PREPARE THE PANS

Butter the 9 inch by 13 inch pan, or place the two 9 inch or 10 inch rounds, preferably with removable bottoms, on a sheet of parchment paper. Trace a circle around them and cut to fit the bottoms of the pans. Lightly butter the sides.

TO PREPARE THE BATTER

In a large bowl, pour the boiling water over the cocoa, whisk until smooth, then allow to cool to room temperature.

Cream together the butter, sugar and vanilla.

In another bowl, sift together the flour, baking soda, baking powder and salt. When the cocoa mixture has cooled to room temperature, add half of it to the creamed mixture. Blend well, scraping the bottom of the bowl. Add half of the flour mixture and blend well again. Add the rest of the cocoa mixture and scrape well again, add the remaining flour mixture. Add the eggs and mix until well incorporated. Pour this mixture into the prepared pan or pans.

TO BAKE

Bake in the fully preheated oven until the cake is firm to the touch. The time needed will depend on the size of your pans. Cool thoroughly before turning out of the pans. Frost the cake with buttercream if desired.

CHERISHED LEMON POPPY SEED CAKE

CAKE BATTER

- BUTTER FOR THE PAN
- ½ CUP FINELY GROUND ALMONDS
- 1 CUP BUTTER
- 3 CUPS SUGAR
- 6 EGGS YOLKS
- 1 CUP SOUR CREAM
- 1 TBS. FRESHLY GRATED LEMON ZEST
- 1 TEASPOON FRESH LEMON JUICE
- ¼ CUP POPPY SEED PASTRY FILLING
- 3 CUPS ALL-PURPOSE FLOUR
- ¼ TEASPOON BAKING SODA
- 6 EGG WHITES

GLAZE

- 2 CUPS POWDERED SUGAR
- JUICE OF ONE LEMON

I TASTE THE SUNSHINE IN THE GRAIN

I taste the sunshine in the grain
Of opulent fields: the dews the rain –
The moonlight shadows softly blent
With sheaves that singing winds have bent
I taste all this when mother bakes
Her wholewheat bread and sunshine cakes.

I taste the sunshine in the loaves
Our oven yields; and with the stove's
Warm bakery scent I taste again
The sunset of a wheatfield when
Our family circle - strange, yet true,
Could eat its cake and have it, too!

- Robert Cary

TO PREPARE THE PAN

Generously butter a 10 inch tube pan. Sprinkle the ground almonds into the pan. Over a piece of waxed paper, tilt the pan in all directions to evenly coat with the nuts.

TO PREPARE THE BATTER

Cream together the butter and sugar. Add the egg yolks, one at a time, and slowly add in the sour cream, mix until smooth. Add the lemon zest, lemon juice and the poppy seed pastry filling. Sift together the flour and the baking soda. Add it to the batter and mix only enough to moisten. In a clean bowl, beat the egg whites until stiff but not dry. Fold them into the batter. Pour the batter into the prepared pan.

TO BAKE

Bake the cake in the fully preheated (350 degree) oven for approximately 40-50 minutes, or until a tooth-pick inserted in the center comes out clean. Cool slightly, then invert the pan onto a cooling rack that is sitting on a piece of waxed paper. Remove the cake from the pan and cool, but glaze the cake while still warm.

TO GLAZE

Beat enough powdered sugar with the fresh lemon juice to make a pourable glaze. While the cake is still warm, drizzle the glaze over the top and allow it to run down the sides of the cake. It will set as it cools.

WARM MILK SPONGE CAKE
WITH MOUSSE FILLING

SPONGE CAKE BATTER

1½ CUPS + 1 TABLESPOON SUGAR

4 WHOLE EGGS

2 EGG YOLKS

2 TEASPOONS VANILLA

¼ TEASPOON SALT

⅔ CUP MILK

2 TABLESPOONS BUTTER

2½ CUPS CAKE FLOUR

1 TABLESPOON BAKING POWDER

MOUSSE FILLING

1 recipe of CREAMY BERRY MOUSSE
see page 294

BUTTERCREAM ICING

1 recipe of SATIN RIBBON BUTTERCREAM
see page 245.

TO MY HUSBAND ON VALENTINE'S DAY

On Valentine's Day my heart will go
Along a quiet path to yesterday,
And find a little grade school room and glow
With recollection of the awkward way
My childhood sweetheart slipped a little cake
Across the aisle. The spice and sugar smell
Returns with swift delight and memories wake
Of days when I was taught to write and spell.
It's true, my love, that you are more romantic
Than the small boy I loved when I was ten,
And your sophistication is gigantic
Compared to his shy awkwardness, back then.
But whenever fresh-made cake's the cynosure,
I've noticed through the years, and you'll agree,
Sophistication's gone, and you're once more
The boy who sat across the aisle from me.

- Grace V. Watkins

Preheat the oven to 200 degrees.

TO PREPARE THE PANS

Place a 14 inch round cake pan, preferably with a removable bottom, on a piece of parchment paper. Trace a circle around the pan and cut to fit. Lightly grease the sides with shortening.

TO PREPARE THE SPONGE CAKE BATTER

Spread the sugar evenly onto a clean sheet pan and gently heat it in the oven until it is warm. Remove the sugar from the oven and turn up the oven to 350 degrees.

In a large bowl of an electric mixer, beat together the whole eggs, egg yolks, vanilla and salt. Slowly beat in the warmed sugar. Turn the mixer to high speed and continue beating for about 10 minutes, or until it turns thick and a light lemon color.

Heat the milk and butter together until the butter is melted and the milk is warm. Sift together the flour and baking powder. Fold the flour mixture into the egg mixture, alternating with the warm milk.

Pour the batter into the prepared pan and bake in the fully preheated oven until golden, or until the cake is firm when touched lightly in the center. Cool the cake thoroughly before removing from the pan.

TO FILL THE CAKE WITH MOUSSE

After the cake has cooled completely, remove it from the pan and carefully remove the parchment paper. Cut the cake evenly with a sharp serrated knife to make three layers. Place one layer back into the pan and spread with ½ of the mousse filling. Place the middle layer of cake on the top and spread with the other ½ of the filling. Place the last layer of cake on the top. Wrap lightly with plastic and chill well or overnight.

TO PREPARE THE CAKE BOARD

If you don't have a plate large enough to hold the cake, you can make a cake board by following the directions in PROPER BAKING PROCEDURES FOR CAKES, under the MAKING A CAKE BOARD heading (page 223).

TO FROST THE CAKE

Following the directions on page 245, prepare one recipe of SATIN RIBBON BUTTERCREAM. Invert the cake onto the prepared cake board. Using a cake knife, frost the sides, Using a cake comb, if you have one, make decorative ridges in the sides. Next, smoothly frost the top, then pipe buttercream around the outside edges.

EVE'S APPLE CAKE

CAKE

3 CUPS ALL-PURPOSE FLOUR

2 CUPS SUGAR

1 TEASPOON BAKING SODA

1 TEASPOON SALT

2 TEASPOONS CINNAMON

1¼ CUPS LIGHT VEGETABLE OIL

3 EGGS

3 CUPS DICED APPLES

1 CUP CHOPPED NUTS

1 CUP CHOPPED RAISINS

NUPTIAL NOTE

The flower girl's six, with freckled face.
She glides down the aisle with elfin grace.
Her smile's pure rapture, her eyes are stars
As organ thunders familiar bars
She's dreaming ahead – but to romance,
To love's sweet witchery? Not a chance!
For a girl, at six, makes no mistake –
The wedding's best part is the wedding cake.

- Ethel Jacobson

Preheat the oven to 350 degrees.

TO PREPARE THE PAN

Lightly grease a 9 inch by 13 inch pan with shortening.

TO PREPARE THE BATTER

In a large bowl, whisk together the flour, sugar, baking soda, salt and cinnamon. In another bowl, place the oil, eggs, diced apple, nuts and raisins. Mix slightly. Mix the dry ingredients with the wet with a large wooden spoon, only enough to moisten. Lightly spread the batter evenly into the prepared pan.

TO BAKE

Bake in the fully preheated oven for 1 hour, until slightly firm to the touch. Serve warm or at room temperature.

SATIN RIBBON BUTTERCREAM

2 CUPS EGG WHITES
3 POUNDS WHITE, GRANULATED SUGAR
WATER TO COVER
3 TO 5 POUNDS COLD BUTTER

In a large bowl of an electric mixer, beat the egg whites until stiff, but not dry.

Put the sugar in a large saucepan and add only enough water to cover. Stir only enough with your finger to make sure the middle is wet.

Bring to a boil and cook until a candy thermometer reads 238 degrees, or is at the softball stage. To check this, drop a few drops of the hot mixture into a glass of cold water. If the mixture dissolves, it needs to boil longer, if it stays together and doesn't dissolve in the water, it is ready.

When the sugar mixture has reached the correct temperature, turn the mixer on 3rd speed and slowly drizzle all the hot sugar mixture into the beaten egg whites. Continue beating for another 5 to 10 minutes to allow the mixture to cool. As the hot mixture is added the consistency of the whites will change and will become runny. Don't worry, the cold butter will firm it up.

Cut the cold butter into thin slivers. Place a towel over the top of your mixer to guard against splashing and carefully, with the mixer still running, slide the cold butter slivers into the outside edge of the bowl. Add only enough of the cold butter pieces until the buttercream starts to thicken. Allow to mix for a few more minutes, then turn off the mixer and run a knife through it to see if it's spreadable. If you like it thicker, add another small amount of cold butter and mix well again. If you add too much butter, it will become too thick and not spread as well. The texture should be satiny smooth and creamy.

NOTE

This butter cream is a very light lemon color because of the butter. Where it matters, you might want to find uncolored butter.

A SMALL BOY AT A WEDDING

The banks of flowers are lost on him,
The organ music too,
The burning candle, gold and still,
Beside each quiet pew.

Unmoved, he watches bride and groom,
His being filled with ache
To reach the rapturous moment when
He tastes the wedding cake.

– Grace V. Watkins

WHERE TIME STANDS STILL

Each state should keep
Time standing still within its border
By saving one old water-mill
In working order.

Then modern folks could see
The ways of pioneers
And ponder what it costs to blaze
Out first frontiers,
The ingenuity it took
To build the wheel,
The hours of work required
To cook a simple meal.

When back in town perhaps
They would appreciate
The courage and the hardihood
That made us great.

- Eloise Wade Hackett

CHAPTER EIGHT

LUSCIOUS CHEESECAKES

WILLIAMS BROTHERS MILLING COMPANY

EST. 1879

WILLIAMS BROTHERS MILLING COMPANY

Williams Brothers Company flour mill was built in 1878-1879 by Charles and Scott Williams. The building, constructed of brick manufactured locally and poplar timbers, was built upon the granite bedrock that runs along the Cuyahoga River through Kent, Ohio. Using the new steel roller mill technology, the Williams Bros. quickly displaced the existing water-powered mill operated by the Kent family.

From its beginning in 1879 until the turn of the century, production slowly grew from approximately 50 to 250 barrels of flour a day. It was during this period that Scott Williams departed from the organization, leaving the management of the mill in the hands of his brother, Charles. Through the early decades of the 1900's, the mill underwent improvements with the installation of new milling equipment, which included the introduction of Allis Chalmbers Rollers. Once again, production increased, and soon the mill was producing 400 barrels of flour a day.

During this period of continuous expansion and improvement, much of the mill's production was sold by Charles throughout the south and southeast to the small grocery trade in 5, 10, and 25 pound branded bags. The Williams Brothers Company developed and promoted several brands at this time which included Perfection Cake, Celestial Cake, Kent Special Cake and Golden Charm Pastry. By 1930, with the mill now under the direction of Charles' son, Dudley, mill production became almost exclusively hi-ration cake flour. New commercial markets in the New York City and New Jersey areas were developed and the mill was operating at full capacity.

The decade of the 1930's saw the installation of Nordyke sifters, purifiers and the construction of concrete wheat storage. The conversion of the mill from steam power to electricity completed this phase of modernization and the Company entered the era of World War II at the capacity of approximately 1,800 cwt. Daily.

For the next thirty years, the Williams Brothers Company enjoyed a period of steadily increasing capacity and volume growth within the commercial cake flour industry. In the 1970's with the decline of the cake flour market imminent, Dudley's son, Charles, embarked on a program to further increase daily production, expand flour storage capacity, develop bulk handling and shipping capacities and expand into growing cookie and cracker markets.

This effort continues today with current daily capacity at approximately 4,000 cwt. Plans are underway to further increase both output and efficiency. The Williams Brothers Company continues to pursue strategies that will ensure it's success as it enters the new millennium.

FIELDS OF GOLD

Our fathers toiled the plains to seek the luring gold!
The epic of their wagin-trains on history's page is told!
Across the western prairies those brave men their way have gone;
Nor dreamed they of the gold which grows where then they hurried on!

For golden fields now spring today – bright harvest fields of wheat!
The countless acres stretch away to where the dim hills meet
The summer sky! – And ev'ry vale and ev'ry swelling rise
Bears yellow grain, where once the trail told of a new emprise!

The fields which ripen 'neath the sun bear Nature's gift of gold!
Not from the rocky ledges won, but sprung from seed and mold!
Gold of the smiling summer day! Gold of the light and air!
No transient vein – no brief assay – but true gold – ev'rywhere!

– Clarence Mansfield Lindsay

PROPER BAKING PROCEDURES FOR CHEESECAKES

TO PREPARE THE CHEESECAKE BATTER

It is easier to mix the cheesecake batter when the cream cheese is at room temperature. Make sure it is thoroughly beaten with the sugar before you add the eggs. Mix everything together thoroughly, scraping the bowl often when adding ingredients.

ADDING THE EGGS

Add the eggs, one at a time, on medium speed, scraping the bowl after each addition. If the mixer is on too high of a speed, it will break down the consistency of the eggs and the cheesecake won't be as light.

ADDING FRESH OR FROZEN FRUIT

If adding fresh fruit, such as berries, select fruit that is not over-ripe. Add the fresh or frozen fruit after you add the eggs and mix only enough to distribute the whole berries evenly throughout the batter.

If you are adding frozen fruit or berries, choose fruit to which no sugar has been added. I like to keep the fruit frozen so that when the cheesecake is cut, there are pretty colorful pieces in each slice.

MULTIPLYING INTO LARGER QUANTITIES

All of the cheesecake recipes, with the exception of pumpkin, can be successfully multiplied by two, three or four. When making more than one pumpkin cheesecake, you multiply the filling times two and multiply the crust and topping by three because it makes three cheesecakes.

TO BAKE THE CHEESECAKE

Bake the cheesecake in the fully preheated oven on a sheet pan to catch any butter that seeps out of the pan during the baking process.

TESTING FOR DONENESS

The cheesecake is ready to be removed from the oven when it has puffed up and is slightly firm when touched in the center. After removal from the oven, allow to settle while you prepare the topping.

TO PREPARE THE TOPPING, BAKE AGAIN AND CHILL UNTIL SET

After the cheesecake has been removed from the oven, mix together all the topping ingredients in a glass bowl. When the cheesecake has settled and the top is once again almost flat, (about 5 minutes or more), spread the topping onto the cheesecake and return it to the oven for another 5 minutes, or until the topping is slightly set.

Carefully remove the cheesecake from the oven and gently run a small knife just around the outside edge. Allow to cool for 5 minutes, then place on a paper towel or a sheet of waxed paper and refrigerate overnight.

SERVING NOTE

The cheesecake needs to be thoroughly chilled before cutting and serving or it will be runny. To serve, carefully remove the rim, running a small knife around the edge if necessary. Run a large knife under the cheesecake to remove it from the bottom pan and slide it onto a large serving plate. Gently score into 16 serving pieces.

To serve, heat a large knife in a pitcher of hot water, wipe dry and slice the cheesecake in half. Place the knife back in the water to clean and heat, wipe dry and cut the first slice. Repeat this process until you have enough servings. Store the remainder in the refrigerator.

If you like cheesecake, thank the ancient Greek bakers, for they originated it, according to Athenaeus, one of the classic Greek authors.

- The Northwestern Miller

ALLURING BERRY CHEESECAKE

CRUST

4 OUNCES BUTTER (1 STICK)
1½ CUPS GROUND VANILLA WAFERS
¼ CUP SUGAR
½ CUP GROUND ALMONDS

TOPPING

2 CUPS SOUR CREAM
¼ CUP SUGAR
1 TEASPOON VANILLA

CHEESECAKE BATTER

2 POUNDS CREAM CHEESE, SOFTENED
1½ CUPS SUGAR
1 TABLESPOON VANILLA
3 TABLESPOONS RASPBERRY
  OR BLACKBERRY LIQUEUR
1 CUP FRESH OR FROZEN RASPBERRIES
  OR BLACKBERRIES
4 LARGE EGGS

TO PREPARE THE CRUST

In a small pan, melt the butter. Mix together the ground vanilla wafers, sugar and ground almonds. Add the melted butter and mix well. Press this mixture up the sides evenly to within 1 inch of the top of a 10 inch spring form pan. Spread the remainder evenly on the bottom of the pan, patting it lightly in place.

TO PREPARE THE FILLING

Thoroughly cream together the cream cheese and sugar. Add the vanilla and the raspberry or blackberry liqueur, scraping the sides of the bowl until well incorporated. On medium speed, add the eggs, one at a time, scraping well after each addition. Add the fresh or frozen raspberries or blackberries and mix only enough to distribute evenly throughout the batter. Pour this batter into the prepared crust.

TO BAKE

Preheat the oven to 350 degrees. Place the cheesecake on a sheet pan and bake in the fully preheated oven for 40 to 50 minutes, or until the cheesecake starts to rise and feels slightly firm in the center. Remove from the oven and let it set while you prepare the topping.

Follow the directions on page 253, PROPER BAKING PROCEDURES FOR CHEESECAKES, under the TO PREPARE THE TOPPING, BAKE AGAIN, AND CHILL UNTIL SET heading.

IN TUNE WITH THE PERFECT

Snow blankets every house-top
Caulks tightly every seam
In eaves and window-sill and door
So snugly, the outer world seems more
Like an enchanted dream.

So I'll bake lovely cheesecakes
To serve with curded cream.
I'll ground a wafer crust light as snow,
Set festive candles, to glow,
With their treaured homing gleam.
Evenings like this, nothing must mar
A perfect world, loaned from afar.

- Kunigunde Duncan

ORANGE ANGELIC CHEESECAKE
OR FRESH LEMON CHEESECAKE

CRUST

4 OUNCES BUTTER (1 STICK)
1½ CUPS GROUND VANILLA WAFERS
¼ CUP SUGAR
½ CUP GROUND ALMONDS OR PECANS

TOPPING

2 CUPS SOUR CREAM
¼ CUP SUGAR
1 TEASPOON VANILLA

CHEESECAKE BATTER

2 POUNDS CREAM CHEESE, SOFTENED
1½ CUPS SUGAR
1 TABLESPOON VANILLA
ZEST FROM 1 ORANGE OR LEMON
JUICE OF 1 ORANGE OR LEMON
4 LARGE EGGS

TO PREPARE THE CRUST

In a small pan, melt the butter. Mix together the ground vanilla wafers, sugar and ground almonds. Add the melted butter and mix well. Press this mixture up the sides evenly to within 1 inch of the top of a 10 inch spring form pan. Spread the remainder evenly on the bottom of the pan, patting it lightly into place.

TO PREPARE THE FILLING

Thoroughly cream together the cream cheese and sugar. Add the vanilla and the lemon zest and juice, scraping the sides of the bowl until well incorporated. On medium speed, add the eggs, one at a time, scraping well after each addition. Pour this batter into the prepared crust.

TO BAKE

Preheat the oven to 350 degrees. Place the cheesecake on a sheet pan and bake in the fully preheated oven for 40 to 50 minutes, or until the cheesecake starts to rise slightly and feels slightly firm in the center. Remove from the oven and let the cheesecake set while you prepare the topping.

Follow the directions on page 253, PROPER BAKING PROCEDURES FOR CHEESECAKES, under the TO PREPARE THE TOPPING, BAKE AGAIN, AND CHILL UNTIL SET heading.

FRANGELICO LACED HAZELNUT CHEESECAKE

CRUST

4 OUNCES BUTTER (1 STICK)
1½ CUPS GROUND VANILLA WAFERS
¼ CUP SUGAR
½ CUP GROUND, TOASTED HAZELNUTS

TOPPING

2 CUPS SOUR CREAM
¼ CUP SUGAR
1 TEASPOON VANILLA

CHEESECAKE BATTER

2 POUNDS CREAM CHEESE, SOFTENED
1½ CUPS SUGAR
1 TABLESPOON VANILLA
2 TABLESPOONS FRANGELICO LIQUEUR
¼ CUP FINELY GROUND,
    LIGHTLY TOASTED HAZELNUTS
4 LARGE EGGS

TO TOAST THE NUTS

Place the hazelnuts on a sheet pan and slowly toast them in a moderate oven for a few minutes or until they start to turn brown. Cool, then remove the skins by rubbing them together. Grind them until fine, then sift ¼ cup to set aside for the filling.

TO PREPARE THE CRUST

In a small pan, melt the butter. Mix together the ground vanilla wafers, sugar and ground hazelnuts. Add the melted butter and mix well. Press this mixture up the sides evenly to within 1 inch of the top of a 10 inch spring form pan. Spread the remainder evenly on the bottom of the pan, patting it lightly in place.

TO PREPARE THE FILLING

Thoroughly cream together the cream cheese and sugar. Add the vanilla, Frangelico and the ¼ cup of finely ground, toasted, sifted hazelnuts, scraping the sides of the bowl until well incorporated. On medium speed, add the eggs, one at a time, scraping well after each addition. Pour this batter into the prepared crust.

TO BAKE

Preheat the oven to 350 degrees. Place the cheesecake on a sheet pan and bake in the fully preheated oven for 40 to 50 minutes or until the cheesecake starts to rise and feels slightly firm in the center. Remove from the oven and let the cheesecake set while you prepare the topping.

Follow the directions on page 253, PROPER BAKING PROCEDURES FOR CHEESECAKES, under the TO PREPARE THE TOPPING, BAKE AGAIN, AND CHILL UNTIL SET heading.

CHOCOLATE KAHLUA CHEESECAKE

CRUST

4 OUNCES BUTTER (1 STICK)
2 CUPS GROUND CHOCOLATE
   WAFER CRUMBS
¼ CUP SUGAR
½ CUP GROUND ALMONDS

TOPPING

2 CUPS SOUR CREAM
¼ CUP SUGAR
1 TEASPOON ALMOND EXTRACT

CHEESECAKE BATTER

3 CUPS FRESH SWEET
3½ OUNCES CHOPPED, SEMI-SWEET
   GUITTARD CHOCOLATE, MELTED
2 POUNDS CREAM CHEESE, SOFTENED
1¼ CUPS SUGAR
3 TO 4 TABLESPOONS KAHLUA
1 TEASPOON VANILLA
¼ TEASPOON SALT
4 LARGE EGGS
2 OUNCES FINELY CHOPPED,
   SEMI-SWEET GUITTARD CHOCOLATE

TO PREPARE THE CRUST

In a small pan, melt the butter. Mix together the ground chocolate wafer crumbs, sugar and the ground almonds. Add the melted butter and mix well. Press this mixture up the sides evenly to within 1 inch of the top of a 10 inch spring form pan. Spread the remainder evenly on the bottom of the pan, patting it lightly in place.

TO PREPARE THE FILLING

Melt the 3½ ounces chopped chocolate on very low heat, or on the top of a double boiler, being careful not to let it scorch. Thoroughly cream together the cream cheese and sugar until smooth. Add the Kahlua and vanilla. With the mixer running on medium speed, beat the melted chocolate into the batter, scraping the sides of the bowl until well incorporated. Add the 2 ounces chopped chocolate. On medium speed, add the eggs, one at a time, scraping well after each addition. Pour this batter into the prepared crust.

TO BAKE

Preheat the oven to 350 degrees. Place the cheesecake on a sheet pan and bake in the fully preheated oven for 40 to 50 minutes, or until the cheesecake starts to rise slightly and feels slightly firm in the center. Remove from the oven and let the cheesecake set while you prepare the topping.

Follow the directions on page 253, PROPER BAKING PROCEDURES FOR CHEESECAKES, under the TO PREPARE THE TOPPING, BAKE AGAIN, AND CHILL UNTIL SET heading.

BUTTERNUT CHEESECAKE

CRUST

I STICK BUTTER, SOFTENED
1½ CUPS GROUND VANILLA WAFERS
¼ CUP SUGAR
½ CUP GROUND PECANS

TOPPING

2 CUPS SOUR CREAM
¼ CUP SUGAR
1 TEASPOON VANILLA

CHEESECAKE BATTER

2 POUNDS CREAM CHEESE, SOFTENED
1½ CUPS SUGAR
1 TABLESPOON VANILLA
1 CUP BUTTERSCOTCH CHIPS
¼ CUP FINELY GROUND PECANS
4 LARGE EGGS

TO PREPARE THE CRUST

In a small pan, melt the butter. Mix together the ground vanilla wafers, sugar and the ½ cup ground pecans. Add the melted butter and mix well. Press this mixture up the sides evenly to within 1 inch of the top of a 10 inch spring form pan. Spread the remainder evenly on the bottom of the pan, patting it lightly in place.

TO PREPARE THE FILLING

Thoroughly cream together the cream cheese and sugar. Add the vanilla. Melt the butterscotch chips on low heat or in the top of a double boiler, being careful not to let them scorch. With the mixer running on medium speed, beat the melted chips into the batter, scraping the sides of the bowl until well incorporated. Add the finely ground pecans. On medium speed, add the eggs, one at a time, scraping well after each addition. Pour this batter into the prepared crust.

TO BAKE

Preheat the oven to 350 degrees. Place the cheesecake on a sheet pan and bake in the fully preheated oven for 40 to 50 minutes, or until the cheesecake starts to rise slightly and feels slightly firm in the center. Remove from the oven and let the cheesecake set while you prepare the topping.

Follow the directions on page 253, PROPER BAKING PROCEDURES FOR CHEESECAKES, under the TO PREPARE THE TOPPING, BAKE AGAIN, AND CHILL UNTIL SET heading.

WORDS FOR HARVEST

There are the autumnal words to sound, like yellow,
The crisp of red and gold – and the sunlight mellow;
The things that we say like husk, and yield, and glory...
The tale that the heart relates of the season's story.
There are the hills and fields from the summer's yearning,
And words that bestir the dream in the wood's gay turning.
But words that break like song above earth's parley
Are sesame, and wheat, and oats, and barley,
Words for goods, to brighten earth's dark hunger –
Joyful words and strong that move all hearts with wonder.

- Helen Maring

SPIRITED PUMPKIN CHEESECAKE

CRUST

4 OUNCES BUTTER (1 STICK)
1¼ CUPS GROUND GINGER SNAPS
¼ CUP SUGAR
¾ CUP GROUND PECANS

TOPPING

2 CUPS SOUR CREAM
¼ CUP SUGAR
1 TEASPOON VANILLA

CHEESECAKE BATTER

2¼ POUNDS CREAM CHEESE,
  SOFTENED
1½ CUPS BROWN SUGAR
⅓ CUP WHITE SUGAR
1 TABLESPOON VANILLA
¾ CUP CANNED OR COOKED
  MASHED PUMPKIN
2 TEASPOONS CINNAMON
1 TEASPOON GINGER
½ TEASPOON NUTMEG
¼ TEASPOON GROUND CLOVES
1 TABLESPOON VANILLA
¼ TEASPOON MACE
3 LARGE EGGS
2 EGG YOLKS

TO PREPARE THE CRUST

In a small pan, melt the butter. Mix together the ground ginger snaps, sugar and ground pecans. Add the melted butter and mix well. Press this mixture up the sides evenly to within 1 inch of the top of a 10 inch spring form pan. Spread the remainder evenly on the bottom of the pan, patting it lightly in place.

TO PREPARE THE FILLING

Thoroughly cream together the cream cheese, brown sugar and the white sugar. Add the pumpkin, cinnamon, ginger, nutmeg, ground cloves, mace and vanilla, scraping the sides of the bowl until well incorporated. On medium speed, add the eggs, one at a time, scraping well after each addition. Add the egg yolks and mix well. Pour this batter into the prepared crust.

TO BAKE

Preheat the oven to 350 degrees. Place the cheesecake on a sheet pan and bake in the fully preheated oven for 40 to 50 minutes, or until the cheesecake starts to rise and feels slightly firm in the center. Remove from the oven and let the cheesecake set while you prepare the topping.

Follow the directions on page 253, PROPER BAKING PROCEDURES FOR CHEESECAKES, under the TO PREPARE THE TOPPING, BAKE AGAIN, AND CHILL UNTIL SET heading.

THANKSGIVING TIME

A twelvemonth gone?
Thanksgiving time is here?

Then spread the damask of white rose design,
Make china, glass and silver brightly shine,
And welcome all the folks whom we hold dear.
Like stalwart Puritan and pioneer,
We set aside this autumn day to dine,
To share the harvest from the goodly cheer.

While sunbeams sparkle on the frosted pane
While flames leap on the hearth, in soft hushed tone
We shall pray around this festive board;
Not only for the bins heaped high with grain,
But for the blessings heart and soul have known,
We shall this day give thanks unto our Lord.

- Beryl Stewart

THE OLD FLOUR MILL

By the clear Chikaskia's gentle tide,
Lonely and weather-beaten and still,
Its great wheel silent by its side,
Yet stands the ancient flour mill.

In a long-gone time its busy hum,
With a rhythm of mellow, homey cheer
Tuned with the bees in the wild plum,
Was once a song to the miller's ear.

The air was hazy and musty sweet
With motes of flour and yellow meal,
Ground from the grist of corn and wheat
In hoppers turned by the huge mill-wheel.

Caught in a fragrant tangle of trees,
By the murmuring waters of the race,
For one with his own long memories
The mill is a peaceful place.

- Maude Greene Princehouse

CHAPTER NINE

COOKIES AND OTHER DESSERT SPECIALTIES

DEDICATED TO THE BAY STATE MILLING COMPANY

EST. 1899

BAY STATE MILLING COMPANY

The man who conceived and spearheaded the founding and development of the Bay State Milling Company was Bernard J. Rothwell. Born in Dublin, Ireland on August 1, 1856, he emigrated to America at the age of ten, and by the age of twelve, he entered the flour brokerage business. He diligently worked his way from bookkeeper to salesmen, to partner. Three years later, young Mr. Rothwell made his first venture into flour milling. In order to obtain control of a regular source of high quality flour, Mr. Rothwell became the head of two milling companies, each of which attained a great deal of success.

THE ROOT MILL - LAWRENCEBURG, INDIANA

In 1895, The Root Mill at Lawrenceburg, Indiana, came up for public auction, and the Rothwell group was the successful bidder. Mr. Rothwell became president and the mill was organized as the Lawrenceburg Roller Mills Company, a prominent leader in the industry for the next 45 years.

THE PORTER MILL - WINONA, MINNEAPOLIS

The original Porter Mill was a 70' by 40,' five-story wood frame building, eventually producing 500 barrels a day in 1881, with the use of both the burr stone and roller processes. After being destroyed by fire, the mill was rebuilt, the capacity increased, and it continued to operate until the demands of the U.S. and foreign market made it necessary to enlarge and improve the operation. Within 12 years, the Bay State Milling Company became regarded as one of the foremost milling concerns in the country, carrying Winona flour into homes across the land.

Lost in another fire in 1911, a new plant was constructed in 1912, complete with modern equipment, 56 double strands of nickel-trimmed grinding rolls, a marble grinding floor, and surrounding walls and columns covered from floor to ceiling with white glazed tile. Sunshine, light and air permeated the mill and all the employees were clad in spotless white suits and caps. The mill is still in operation today, selling commercial flour to institutions across the nation.

THE L.C. LYSLE COMPANY - LEAVENWORTH

Bay State expanded its milling operations outside Winona in the spring of 1954, when it purchased the idle L.C. Lysle Milling Company at Leavenworth, Kansas. Founded in 1874, the mill was one of the original pioneer flour milling organizations in the Kansas area.

THE LA GRANGE MILL - RED WING, MISSISSIPPI

Founded in 1877, located on the Mississippi River, the La Grange Mill had a colorful history, extending over a period of great revolutions in the milling industry. In 1961, Bay State acquired the Red Wing plant from the La Grange Mills which had been in existence for 84 years. In 1973, the almost 100 year old mill was destroyed by fire.

THE HAYDEN MILL - TEMPE, ARIZONA

Like a giant castle, Hayden's Flour Mill stands guard at the foot of the Mill Avenue Bridge watching over all who enter the city. The mill is Arizona's oldest manufacturing establishment, built from adobe in 1872 by

Charles Trumbull Hayden, pioneer merchant and town developer. The original flour mill was operated by a water wheel turned by water power from the old Hayden ditch dug around the foot of Tempe Butte. Pima and Maricopa Indians were the first to sell their grain to the mill followed by the Mormon pioneers.

The mill had changed hands several times during its 100 year history, but when it was consolidated under the roof of the Bay State Milling Company, in 1981, it was owned by Charles C. Hayden, grandson of the original owner. Flour brands at that time included Rose, Family Kitchen, Tulip, Tortilla, Navajo Maid, Crown-O-Gold, Arizona Maid and La Paloma-all of which were consumed by the State of Arizona. Bay State felt it important to retain the Hayden name and the family tradition.

Flours produced by Bay State are marketed throughout the United States. With its expanded milling capacity, the firm also entered in the foreign market, shipping its products to the Dominican Republic, the West Indies, Guatemala, Costa Rica, Nicaragua, Panama, Venezuela, Holland, Norway and Denmark.

The Bay State Milling Company today is the sixth largest flour producer in the United States, ranking second in the milling of whole wheat and rye. Currently they operate eight mills, which are located in Tempe, Arizona; Tolleson, Arizona; Indiantown, Florida; Winona, Minnesota; Clifton, New Jersey; and Mooreville, North Carolina.

The Company has been controlled throughout its history by the Rothwells. They celebrated their centennial in the year 1999.

PROPER BAKING PROCEDURES
FOR COOKIES & PUDDINGS, ETC.

PREPARING THE PANS

The best pans to use when baking cookies are the heavy professional sheet pans. They come in full and half sheet sizes. They maintain and distribute the heat evenly, giving the cookies a uniform bake.

To prepare the pans, line them with parchment paper which can be purchased from a cooking shop or a bakery. Ask them if you can by a dozen sheets the next time you make cookies. They will keep their shape and bake up nicer than those baked on greased pans. If your parchment paper is full-sheet size, cut the sheets in half. The paper can be used again by flipping it over.

MIXING THE DOUGH

Thoroughly cream the butter with the sugar before adding the other ingredients or the cookies may have holes. Scrape the bottom of the bowl after each addition. To keep the cookies light, do not over-mix the dough.

HANDLING THE DOUGH

Overworking the dough causes toughness. If you are rolling out the dough to cut it into fanciful shapes, space your cuts as close together as possible. Every time the dough is re-rolled it becomes tougher.

PANNING THE COOKIES

Pan cookies of the same size on the same baking sheet so they will bake evenly. Space them evenly apart so they can spread.

FOR PUDDINGS, ETC.

Puddings are very popular and as with other desserts, careful preparation is necessary to obtain the best results. Follow the recipe directions carefully. Bake the puddings at the recommended temperatures, too high of a heat will cause them to curdle. Cream puffs need the instant high heat in order for them to rise properly, so begin heating your oven in plenty of time so that it reaches the correct temperature.

GINGERBREAD MEN

Yesterday's grandmothers seemed to know when
Children were hungry for gingerbread men,
And into the oven along with the pies
Went pans full of men with currants for eyes.

But grandmother's lives must be busier now,
Or maybe they never had time to learn how
Alluring are spicy brown men who just beg
A child to bite off a crisp arm or leg.

Alas for the youngsters who never have known
A "baked-just-for you, dear," man of their own!
And how lucky were we whose grandmothers made
Our gingerbread men in an endless parade!

– Eloise Wade Hackett

SHORTBREAD HEARTS

COOKIE DOUGH

1 CUP BUTTER (2 STICKS), ROOM TEMPERATURE
¾ CUP SUGAR
1 TEASPOON VANILLA
1½ CUPS ALL-PURPOSE FLOUR
½ CUP CORNSTARCH
¼ TEASPOON SALT

CHOCOLATE DIP

8 OUNCES CHOPPED, SEMI-SWEET CHOCOLATE
1 TABLESPOON VEGETABLE OIL

WHITE CHOCOLATE DIP

8 OUNCES WHITE CHOCOLATE, CHOPPED
1 TABLESPOON VEGETABLE OIL

YOUNG APPRAISAL

My mother's keen.
She fills jars
With shortbread
Hearts and stars,
And leaves them
Handy on a shelf
Where a boy
Can help himself.
When I kiss her –
That's the price –
My mother smells
Like cookie spice.

-Ethel Romig Fuller

TO PREPARE THE DOUGH

Cream together the butter and sugar until light and fluffy. Add the vanilla. Sift together the flour, cornstarch and salt. Add it to the creamed mixture and mix thoroughly. On a lightly floured board, briefly kneed the dough to bind. Chill the dough if necessary. Preheat the oven to 350 degrees.

Roll out the dough, ¼ inch thick, on a lightly floured board. Cut into heart shapes and space them evenly onto a half sheet pan lined with parchment paper, or a lightly greased cookie sheet. Using a fork, poke two rows of traditional shortbread markings into the dough.

TO BAKE

Bake in the preheated oven for 5-8 minutes or until lightly golden around the edges. Let cool on the pan for a brief moment, then carefully remove them from the sheet pan and place them onto a rack to cool.

PREPARING THE CHOCOLATE DIPS

In two small separate pans, over very low heat, very gently melt the dark chocolate and the white chocolate until smooth. Remove from the heat and stir in the vegetable oil.

Clear a shelf in your refrigerator and line it with parchment paper or waxed paper. Dip the cooled cookie edges into the chocolate dips to cover the edge or edges, or drizzle the chocolate from a fork in a lacy pattern. Cool on the paper in the refrigerator until set. Peel off carefully.

TEA THYME LEMON COOKIES

YIELD: 36 SMALL COOKIES

COOKIE DOUGH

1 CUP BUTTER (2 STICKS)

1¼ CUPS SUGAR

2 EGGS

1 TABLESPOON FRESH GRATED LEMON ZEST

2¾ CUPS ALL-PURPOSE FLOUR

2 TEASPOONS BAKING POWDER

2 TABLESPOONS FINELY CHOPPED FRESH THYME
   OR 2 TEASPOONS DRY THYME

ROLLING SUGAR

¼ CUP SUGAR

Most glamour girls of 17th century England carried handkerchiefs on which were inscribed recipes for bread, cake and cookie baking.

– The Northwestern Miller

TO PREPARE THE DOUGH

Thoroughly cream together the butter and the 1¾ cup sugar. Add the eggs and freshly grated lemon peel and mix well.

Mix together the flour, baking powder and thyme. Add to the creamed mixture and mix well to blend. Chill the dough to make it easier to handle.

Preheat the oven to 350 degrees.

Divide the dough into 36 small balls. Roll the balls in the ¼ cup sugar and space evenly on a half-sheet pan that has been lined with parchment paper or a lightly greased cookie sheet. Flatten slightly with the palm of your hand.

TO BAKE

Bake for 12 to 15 minutes or until lightly golden. Carefully remove them from the sheet pan and place them on a rack to cool.

KID GLOVE COOKIES

278

COOKIE DOUGH

⅔ CUP BUTTER

1½ CUPS SUGAR

2 EGGS

1 TEASPOON FINELY GRATED LEMON ZEST

JUICE OF ONE LEMON

3 CUPS ALL-PURPOSE FLOUR

2 TEASPOONS BAKING POWDER

1 TEASPOON SALT

POWDERED SUGAR FOR DUSTING

TO PREPARE THE DOUGH

Cream together the butter and the sugar. Add the eggs, the finely grated lemon zest and the lemon juice.

Sift together the flour, baking powder and the salt. Mix the flour mixture with the creamed mixture only enough to blend. Wrap the dough in plastic wrap and chill thoroughly.

Preheat the oven to 350 degrees.

Roll the dough out onto a lightly floured board to ¼ inch thickness. Cut with a hand-shaped cookie cutter or any other decoratively shaped cutter. Carefully place on a sheet pan that has been lined with parchment paper or a very lightly greased cookie sheet.

TO BAKE

Bake for 5 to 8 minutes or until lightly golden. Carefully remove to a cooling rack. Allow to cool completely. Using a sifter, dust with powdered sugar.

BAKING COOKIES

As my small twins make cookie dough,
Jane splatters egg yolk on the floor,
But Jean stoops down to mop it up
With her white pinafore.

To mix a few ingredients,
The twins work on the double-quick;
Then Jane rolls cookies paper thin,
But Jane prefers them thick.

Jane bakes her cookies to the hue
Of country butter freshly churned,
But Jean bakes hers until they are
Unquestionably burned.

Now while I watch my cherubs clean
The dribble sink and littered spaces,
I think my twins look beautiful
With flour upon their faces.

- Beryl Stewart

A PRECIOUS GIFT

Give a child bright-colored jars
Filled with sugared cookie stars,
And he'll have memories to sustain
His heart in hours of grief and pain—
Planetary memories of
Laughter, home, a mother's love.

– Ethel Romig Fuller

WISH UPON GINGER STARS

COOKIE DOUGH

1 CUP BUTTER (2 STICKS)
1½ CUPS LIGHT BROWN SUGAR,
   LIGHTLY PACKED
¼ CUP DARK MOLASSES
1 EGG, ROOM TEMPERATURE
2⅔ CUPS ALL-PURPOSE FLOUR
2 TEASPOONS GINGER
1½ TEASPOONS CLOVES
1½ TEASPOONS CINNAMON
1½ TEASPOONS SODA
½ TEASPOON SALT
WHITE SUGAR FOR SPRINKLING

TO PREPARE THE DOUGH

Melt the butter and let it cool.

Combine the brown sugar, molasses and egg. Add the melted, cooled butter.

Sift together the flour, ginger, cloves, cinnamon, soda and salt. Mix the wet ingredients with the dry.

Divide the dough into ⅓'s. Roll each ⅓ thickly between two sheets of waxed paper. Chill the dough well in the freezer for 1 hour or in the refrigerator overnight.

After it is well chilled, preheat the oven to 350 degrees.

Working with one piece at a time, remove the waxed paper and roll the dough out to ¼ inch thick. Cut with a star cookie cutter and place on a half-sheet pan that has been lined with parchment paper or a lightly greased cookie sheet. Sprinkle with sugar.

TO BAKE

Bake the cookie stars in the fully preheated oven for 6 to 8 minutes, or until lightly browned but soft. Cool slightly before removing with a spatula to a cooling rack.

SUNFLOWER SESAME SEED COOKIES

COOKIE DOUGH

½ CUP BUTTER (1 STICK)

1 CUP FIRMLY PACKED BROWN SUGAR

¾ CUP WHITE SUGAR

2 EGGS

1 TEASPOON VANILLA

1½ CUPS ALL-PURPOSE FLOUR

1 TEASPOON BAKING SODA

¾ TEASPOON SALT

3 CUPS QUICK COOKING ROLLED OATS

1 CUP RAW SUNFLOWER SEEDS

½ CUP RAW SESAME SEEDS

TO PREPARE THE DOUGH

Cream together the butter with the brown and white sugars. Add the eggs and vanilla.

Sift together the flour, baking soda and salt. Mix the flour mixture into the creamed mixture. Add the rolled oats, sunflower seeds and sesame seeds and mix again to blend.

Preheat the oven to 350 degrees.

Roll the dough into small balls and space evenly onto a sheet pan that has been lined with parchment paper or a lightly greased cookie sheet. Flatten them out slightly with the palm of your hand.

TO BAKE

Bake in the preheated oven for 8-12 minutes, or until lightly golden. Cool slightly before removing with a spatula to a cooling rack.

PLAIN OR FANCY

Cookie jars these days are fancy affairs,
Animals, houses or comical fellows.
They're used as an accent in kitchen decor
And rival the rainbow with reds,
Blues and yellows.

But as for contents, the best jar I've known
Is hid by a door at which memory knocks,
A plain stoneware jar in grandmother's pantry,
Full of fresh gingersnaps, hermits, or rocks.

– Eloise Wade Hackett

WHITE CHOCOLATE MACADAMIA NUT COOKIES

COOKIE DOUGH

2¼ CUPS ALL-PURPOSE FLOUR

1 TEASPOON BAKING SODA

½ TEASPOON SALT

1 CUP BUTTER (2 STICKS)

¾ CUP WHITE SUGAR

¾ CUP BROWN SUGAR

1 TEASPOON VANILLA

2 EGGS

1 (12 OUNCE) PACKAGE OF WHITE CHOCOLATE CHIPS

3½ OUNCES COARSELY CHOPPED MACADAMIA NUTS

TO PREPARE THE DOUGH

Combine the flour, soda and salt. In a large bowl, cream together the butter, white and brown sugar and the vanilla. Beat in the eggs, one at a time, scraping well after each addition.

Add the flour mixture to the wet ingredients to blend. Add the white chocolate chips and the chopped nuts.

TO BAKE

Drop by spoonfuls onto a half-sheet pan lined with parchment paper or a lightly greased cookie sheet. Bake in the preheated oven (350 degrees)for about 7 minutes, or until light golden. Carefully remove to a cooling rack.

COOKIE DAY

Of all the happy days there are
That fill our hearts with glee
When mother fills the cookie jar
Is happiest for me.

Her heaps of flour, light as floss
And white as falling snow,
She'll mix and sift and lightly toss
Into a roll of dough.

And this she'll knead and knead again;
Roll out tillbroad and thin:
Sprinkle with spicy sweets, and then
Cut with a cookie tin.

The heated oven open wide
And takes the shallow tray;
Sweet odors billow, like a tide,
To advertise the day.

Then out they come, delicious , tan,
The circle and the star,
Set out to cool beside the pan
Before they reach the jar.

And ah, it's such a joy to find
That jar upon a shelf
Where, day by day, as I am inclined
I'm free to help myself.

- Edwin T. Reed

BOYFRIEND BROWNIES

BROWNIE BATTER

> ¼ CUP ALL-PURPOSE FLOUR
>
> 2 TABLESPOONS COCOA POWDER
>
> 1 TEASPOON BAKING POWDER
>
> ½ TEASPOON SALT
>
> 2 OZ. SEMI-SWEET CHOCOLATE, CHOPPED
>
> 3 OZ. UNSWEETENED CHOCOLATE, CHOPPED
>
> 4 TABLESPOONS BUTTER (½ STICK)
>
> 3 EGGS
>
> 1 CUP SUGAR
>
> 1 TEASPOON VANILLA
>
> ¼ CUP SOUR CREAM

Baking powder once came wrapped in three seperate packages, containing calcium phosphate, bicarbonate of soda, and cornstarch. The house-wife, when preparing dough or batter, mixed them all up together herself.

– The Northwestern Miller

OPTIONAL ICING

1 recipe of CHOCOLATE TRUFFLE TORTE ICING, See page 235 and 236.

> ½ CUP CHOPPED WALNUTS (OPTIONAL)

Preheat the oven to 350 degrees.

TO PREPARE THE PAN

Lightly butter a 9 inch square pan, or line the bottom with parchment paper and butter the sides.

TO PREPARE THE BATTER

Sift together the flour, cocoa powder, baking powder and salt. In a bowl, over hot but not boiling water, gently heat together the chopped chocolate, chopped unsweetened chocolate and the butter until melted.

Beat together the eggs, sugar and vanilla. Mix the flour into the egg mixture, ⅓ at a time, alternating it with the chocolate mixture. Carefully spread the brownie batter into the prepared pan.

TO BAKE

Bake in the preheated oven for 25 minutes, or until the sides are starting to set. Cool before icing.

TO ICE THE BROWNIES

Prepare one recipe of the CHOCOLATE TRUFFLE TORTE ICING on page 236. After the brownies have cooled to room temperature, spread them with the cooled icing. Run the knife back and forth in opposite directions to make an attractive pattern in the icing. Sprinkle with the chopped walnuts.

LEMON BARS

CRUST

- 1 CUP BUTTER (2 STICKS)
- ½ CUP POWDERED SUGAR
- ½ TEASPOON SALT
- 2 CUPS ALL-PURPOSE FLOUR

FILLING

- 4 EGGS
- 2 CUPS SUGAR
- 2 TEASPOONS FRESH LEMON ZEST
- ¼ CUP FRESH LEMON JUICE
- ½ TEASPOON BAKING POWDER
- 2 TABLESPOONS ALL-PURPOSE FLOUR

TOPPING

- ¾ CUP POWDERED SUGAR

THE BAKERY DISPLAY

There are lemon bars and cookies
And sugar-glazed "claws"
And huddles of fragrant,
Brown-crusted bread,

And grown-ups as eager
As juveniles pause
To choose from the good things
So temptingly spread.

There are pies of all kinds:
Open faced and crusted,
With mouth-watering pools
Of rich juices oozing;

And cakes richly frosted
And jelly rolls dusted
Thickly with sugar,
All for our difficult choosing.

- Maude Rene Princehouse

TO PREPARE THE CRUST

Preheat oven to 350 degrees.

Cream together the butter and powdered sugar. Cut in the salt and the flour until mealy. Gently press this mixture into the bottom of a lightly buttered 9 inch by 13 inch pan.

TO BAKE

Partially bake the crust for 8 minutes while you prepare the filling.

TO PREPARE THE FILLING

Mix the filling ingredients together in the order given. Pour the filling into the partially baked crust.

TO BAKE

Bake for 20 to 25 minutes, or until lightly golden. Cool.

With a sifter, dust with powdered sugar before cutting into bars.

STARRY DREAM CREAM PUFFS

PUFF DOUGH

½ CUP (1 STICK) BUTTER, CUT INTO PIECES
1 CUP WATER
1 CUP ALL-PURPOSE FLOUR
4 EGGS, BEATEN

"Flour" and "flower" are closely related, since "flour" is derived from the French "fleur de farine," which means flower of the meal, or, more loosely translated, the best of the grain when ground.

CREAM PUFF FILLING

2 CUPS WHIPPED CREAM
½ CUP POWDERED SUGAR
1 TABLESPOON VANILLA
CHOCOLATE TRUFFLE
TORTE TOPPING, PAGE 235
1 CUP TOASTED ALMONDS

- The Northwestern Miller

Preheat the oven to 400 degrees.

In a large, non-aluminum pan, heat the butter and water together until the butter melts and the water comes to a rolling boil.

Remove from the heat and whisk in the flour. Return to low heat and continue to whisk vigorously for one minute, until the mixture is very smooth, pulls away from the sides of the pan and forms a ball.

Remove from the heat and whisk in the beaten eggs, all at once. Beat until smooth.

Pipe the dough to form small balls onto a sheet-pan that has been lined with parchment paper. Bake in the fully preheated oven for 40 minutes, or until golden. Cool completely before cutting the tops to fill.

TO PREPARE THE FILLING

While the cream puffs are cooling, prepare the Chocolate Truffle Torte Topping as described on page 235 and 236.

Lightly toast the almonds on a sheet pan in a moderate oven. Cool.

Whip the whipping cream, powdered sugar and vanilla together until it holds stiff peaks. Cut the tops off the cream puffs and set them aside. Using a pastry bag with a large star tip, pipe the whipping cream into the cream puffs. Place the tops on, drizzle with the chocolate topping and sprinkle with toasted almonds.

ANGEL WINGS CREAM

CREAM

> 2 TABLESPOONS UNFLAVORED GELATIN
> ½ CUP COLD WATER
> 1¾ CUPS LIGHT CREAM
> 1 CUP SUGAR
> 1½ CUPS SOUR CREAM
> 1 TEASPOON VANILLA

GARNISH

> FRESH BERRIES

1 recipe of SHORTBREAD HEART cookies page 274.

HOW VERY BLEST!

No bluer blue, than flax, could be –
A scrap of sky's infinity.
Through fragrant buckwheat blossoms run
The pink where of June draws are spun.

Wind, ruffling barley, sets in motion
A green and silver inland ocean.
Where corn ripens, a supernal
Gold on cored in every kernal.

O the colors, summer yields
To eyes that look upon grain fields;
To eyes, to hearts! How blest, the man
Beholding harvests flower again!

-Ethel Romig Fuller

TO PREPARE THE CREAM

In a small bowl, soak the gelatin in the cold water until the water is absorbed.

Gently heat together the light cream and sugar until the sugar dissolves. Whisk the gelatin into the hot cream. Remove from the heat.

In a large bowl, whisk together the sour cream and vanilla. Fold the light cream into the sour cream mixture. Pour into your favorite mold or serving glasses. Chill thoroughly to set.

TO GARNISH AND SERVE

Garnish with fresh berries and serve with tea cookies, such as SHORTBREAD HEARTS, on page 274.

CREAMY BERRY MOUSSE

BERRY MOUSSE

2 CUPS FROZEN BLACKBERRIES

¼ CUP RESERVED JUICE
  FROM THE THAWED BERRIES

1 TABLESPOON UNFLAVORED GELATIN

8 OUNCES CREAM CHEESE, SOFTENED

½ CUP SUGAR

1¼ CUPS HEAVY CREAM

1 TEASPOON VANILLA

GARNISH

1 CUP HEAVY CREAM

4 TABLESPOONS POWDERED SUGAR

1 TEASPOON VANILLA

Ancient Romans ate their gala dinners to the smell of perfume. Slaves stood by at their colorful banquets and sprayed the air with different scents, varying with the delicacy of the food being served. The cushions on which guests reclined were changed with each course to match the color of the tidbit, main course, or dessert they were going to eat.

– The Northwesten Miller

TO PREPARE THE MOUSSE

Thaw the berries in a colander allowing the juice to drain into a bowl. Reserve ¼ cup of the juice and pour it into a small pan. Stir in the gelatin and set aside to soften, about 5 minutes. Gently heat the juice until the gelatin dissolves. Set aside to cool.

Beat the softened cream cheese with the sugar. Add one cup of the thawed berries and mix well. With the mixer running, slowly add the dissolved gelatin mixture. Fold in by hand, the other cup of the thawed blackberries.

Whip the heavy cream with the vanilla until it holds soft peaks. Fold it into the mousse and spoon it into individual serving glasses. Chill if not serving right away.

TO GARNISH

Beat the heavy cream with the powdered sugar and vanilla until it holds soft peaks. Pipe it onto the mouse before serving.

GRANDMA REDFERN'S RICE PUDDING

RICE PUDDING

½ CUP UNCOOKED REGULAR RICE

1 CUP WATER

2½ CUPS MILK

2 EGGS, SEPARATED

¼ CUP SUGAR

½ CUP RAISINS

1 TABLESPOON VANILLA

½ TEASPOON SALT

MERINGUE

2 EGG WHITES

¼ TEASPOON CREAM OF TARTAR

½ TEASPOON VANILLA

¼ CUP SUGAR

RICE PUDDING

Grandmother made it,
Spanking good,
Baked in a range
She stoked with wood,
And we've gone fancier,
We've gone arty
Making desserts
That were far less hearty
So for tonight
Here's a warm, brown dream
Rice pudding, rich
With raisins and cream!

- Ethel Jacobson

Preheat the oven to 350 degrees.

TO PREPARE THE PUDDING

Cook the rice with the water in a medium saucepan over low heat until the water is absorbed, about 20 minutes.

In a large bowl, beat together the milk, eggs, sugar, raisins, vanilla and salt.

Mix in the cooked rice. Pour into a buttered 1½ quart casserole dish. Place the rice pudding on a sheet pan and bake in the preheated oven for 1½ hours, or until the liquid is absorbed and a toothpick inserted into the center comes out clean.

Remove from the oven. Leave the oven temperature at 350 degrees while you prepare the meringue.

TO MAKE THE MERINGUE

Make the meringue by beating the egg whites with the cream of tartar and vanilla until it holds soft peaks. Gradually beat in the sugar until stiff peaks form and the sugar is dissolved. Using a pastry bag with a large tip, pipe swirls on the warm pudding. Return to the oven and bake about 15 minutes, or until the meringue is golden brown. Cool out of drafts. Serve warm or cold.

MILL IN WINTER

The great wheel that in summertime
Was want to turn so slow
Stands motionless, a handy place
For icicles to grow.
The millrace now is bridged with ice
And hidden under snow,
Yet underneath the winter sheath
The ear discerns, below,
The sound of summer's sure approach
In the stream's unceasing flow.

– Eloise Wade Hackett

A TOUR THROUGH THE MILL OF TODAY

THE FISHER BLACKFOOT MILL

In January 1999, flour production began at the most modern conventional mill in North America: The Fisher Mill in Blackfoot, Idaho. Located 200 miles east of Boise, the state's capitol, this facility combines age-tested techniques of flour milling with technology-driven improvements in flexibility, efficiency, and product quality. It is also large, capable of producing 1.7 million pounds of flour daily.

The mill is situated in the middle of a major wheat growing region in order to receive wheat directly from the fields of Idaho and southern Montana. Here, wheat is processed into over thirty blends of flour in accordance with the needs of Fisher's many customers throughout the Western United States and selected foreign markets. To better serve these markets, extensive research and testing were included in the facility's construction to ensure exceptional functionality.

Blackfoot's high-tech features begin with the building itself, which consists of reinforced concrete, poured not in the usual floor by floor manner, but as a continuous and integral unit over a period of 120 hours. This innovative construction places great emphasis on structural integrity and strategic arrangement of staging components to support state-of-the-art processing techniques: from receiving of the just harvested wheat, to converting raw wheat to flour, to shipping the finished product by rail to major markets. All these components are linked by a sophisticated computer system that requires a small but highly trained staff of technicians for optimum operation.

Even with these important technological advances, some things don't change. Millers and bakers of today continue to focus on the amount of protein contained in the flour because consistent protein levels constitute the basis for uniformity in the finished flour product. And this concern starts in the wheat fields with the buying of wheat. The overall objective for the Fisher buyer is to select wheat with the highest quality of protein without sacrificing bushel yield for the farmer. To achieve this important standard, mill personnel first test five-pound samples of wheat to establish yield and protein levels, and then bake these samples to determine the flour's baking characteristics.

After wheat has been selected that reaches Fisher's high standards of consistency and quality, it is stored by class, variety, and protein level. These resulting divisions are then blended to meet the exacting requirements of a wide range of customers-from large grocery chains and specialty food manufacturers like pizza and tortilla makers-to retail bakeries and gourmet bakers.

As noted above, Blackfoot is the quintessential "origin mill," positioned right in the middle of wheat country. Because of this ideal location, most grain is brought to the mill directly by truck, where it is unloaded and put through several cleaning steps. The first involves the use of "separators" which discard large rocks, sticks, and other debris from the raw wheat, followed by a more refined air suspension process that removes the remaining smaller pebbles. The entire procedure is controlled and monitored by a system of computer operated scales that determine the exact amount of "dockage," the cleanings removed from the wheat prior to milling. This ensures that the precise amount of good quality wheat is being retained, rather than discarded.

After cleaning, the wheat is moved to a stage referred to as "tempering." This step is the beginning of the milling process, wherein microwave technology is used to determine the exact amount of water to maintain consistent dampness of the wheat kernels to be ground. Wheat will remain in the temper bins for 16 to 24 hours, where it will mellow to facilitate the crushing and grinding operation referred to as "the break." A second feature of the advanced Blackfoot tempering system is an additional temper that is used 45 minutes prior to the "first break," or grind. This helps keep the coat of the wheat kernel in tact so that a minimum amount of high ash flour is produced. Immediately following tempering, the wheat is sent through a cleaning machine called the "scourer," which functions to remove what millers call "bees wing," a very thin membrane from the outer part of the kernel.

Now the cleaned and conditioned wheat is ready to be milled. At Blackfoot, the grinding and crushing operation is carried out with the help of a new "double high" design mechanism, which uses two grinding steps before each sifting step in order to allow more flour to be produced with much less sifter surface and a smaller building. The sifters themselves consist of eight large stainless steel boxes, with laser sensors to detect even a slight dusting of flour that would indicate a choked condition or disconnection.

Flour mills require substantial height because the crushed and ground wheat needs to be refined repeatedly in order to become finished flour. Using gravity to advantage, the newly ground wheat is pneumatically lifted to the top floor, where it then descends through a series of sifters which separate finer flour particles from the larger bran particles into three classes: coarsest, medium, or "middlings," and the finest, known as "first break flour." At the Blackfoot facility, operators are able to monitor production carefully through an on-line NIR (near infrared reflectance) machine. This device constantly measures the actual flour moisture, protein, and ash, enabling the operating miller to monitor changes in the process and make necessary adjustments to maintain quality.

The ground wheat is then moved to a unique flour blending system that gives Fisher millers a significant advantage over other millers. This system has the ability to take flour from any bin and blend it with flour from other bins in any ratio desired. High-tech computers read the miller's "recipe," and produce the exact proportions ordered. This capability allows Fisher Mills to customize flours for all of its many exacting customers.

Consumption of flour products has been rising steadily in the United States over the past fifteen years, and Fisher intends to meet this demand by offering a variety of high quality products to its customers. Whether the requirement is flour for tortillas, pizza, wraps to contain new entries into our increasingly varied American cuisine, or organic products, the modern mill at Blackfoot will be selecting and processing the best wheat to make these abundant choices possible.

THE MILLER'S SONG

I think I can hear the miller's lad
Go singing up the hill.
And over and over I seem to hear
And I echo the old refrain:
"Turn, turn my wheel, turn once again
And grind my shinning grain,

For your yellow gold is all I hold
Yet not with care I;
I laugh and sing, an uncrowned king,
And let the world go by."

- Florence Jones Hadley

BREAD AND BEAUTY

When moonlight touched to beauty all the field
Of beamy spear on spear,
Up through the silver night, up to the moon
I heard this song rise clear:

We are the army of the wheat. We have battled through the ages
To set our signal in the skies, our story on earth's pages.
Winds are our boon confederates, rain and sun are of these,
And the slow change of seasons rolls out our prophecies.

The grainaries hold our secret, -ah, impatient to reveal
That the lord of all progression is the lord of the turning wheel!
Two utmost needs of man there are for which we rally and strive:
Bread for his body, - beauty to keep his soul alive.
And as long as man is man, as far as the feet of man shall tread,
The flowers of the wheat shall blossom, and the mouth of the world be fed.

So in the piercing sweetness of a night,
In mist of dews upspringing,
I heard the conquering army of the wheat,
The host of beauty singing.

- Agnes Lee

ACKNOWLEDGEMENTS

It takes the help and gifted talents of many people to put a project of this size together. I would like to thank everyone individually and collectively who opened their archives, doors, cupboards and hearts.

My sincere appreciation goes to the Seattle Public Library, for storing the volumes of The Northwestern Miller and The American Miller, and particularly the staff of the Magazines and Periodicals department for ordering and reordering. Special thanks to Martin Burgess, who has been very helpful and supportive throughout the years and to Debora Jacobs, City Librarian & CEO, for the beautiful letter she wrote with Andrea Addison on the book's behalf.

I would like to thank Mr. Michael Ford, V P Publisher of Miller Publishing Company, formerly The Northwestern Miller, for the use of the materials. To my knowledge, there are only two near-complete sets of The Northwestern Miller, one of which is housed in the Seattle Public Library, the other, recently found in the Milling and Baking News Archives (the former office of The Northwestern Miller) and donated to the University of Minnesota. It was only after years of laboriously and lovingly gathering poems, photographs, illustrations and borders for this book, that I found that the Seattle volumes had been donated to the library by the Fisher Flouring Mills Co. Inc.

A special thanks to Bill Krippaehne, President & CEO of Fisher Companies, for the genuine words of encouragement when I first brought in the manuscript, and for his continued support throughout the years, as well as thanks to the late Terry Barrons, President of Fisher Flouring Mills Inc. and Chris Wheeler, Vice President Corporate Communications, Fisher Companies Inc.

I would like to convey my deep gratitude to the late Executive Vice President of the Millers' National Federation, Mr. Herman Steen, who spent many of his retirement years writing his series of books: Flour Milling In America, Millers' National Federation, and The O.W. Fisher Heritage.

I would like to thank Mr. Roy Henwood, Past President of the Millers' National Federation, (recently merged to form the North American Millers' Association) for being so generous with his knowledge, and to Betsy Faga, the current President of the North American Millers' Association for her continued support and the wonderful letter she wrote on the association's behalf.

Sincere thanks to the presidents and vice presidents of the milling companies for supporting me in this romantic endeavor with their heart-felt enthusiasm.

With deepest appreciation I would like to thank Master Baking Instructor Ernie E. Kimberland. A member of the American Society of Baking Engineers, Mr. Kimberland worked for a number of years in the wholesale and retail shops in the Pacific Northwest. He earned an Applied Arts and Science Degree in Vocational Education, graduated from the American Institute of Baking and became a baking instructor at the college level. And to his partner, the late Don Bullington, thanks to the two of you for being such incredible instructors and teaching me the science of baking.

Thanks to my wonderfully amazingly friends and associates, Shelley Odegard, Cooper Edens, Sacheverell Darling, Mark Gordon, Dave Emery, Robert Hayes, John Papajani, Joe Tschida, Doug Fast and Bob Cumbow, for being who you are, and for embracing the book and blessing it with your special talents and gifts. Thank you for putting your heart and soul into it, for weaving such a beautifully romantic tale, and making it such a wonderful journey.

ACKNOWLEDGEMENTS

To Steve Johnson, thanks for always being there when I needed you, for your trust, for talking me into buying a computer and having the patience to show me how to use it. It is to all the above-mentioned that I am forever indebted, for without them and their generous contributions, this book would not have been possible.

And thanks to James Malevitsis, owner of the Ponti and Adriatica restaurants, and Earl Owens, Corporate Chef of Consolidated Restaurants, for writing beautiful letters on the books behalf.

To my mentor, Oma, with cookie and cake smells throughout the house, you were the most loving grandmother, mother, mother-in-law and friend that anyone could ever have. You are dearly missed.

To my father, Dr. Melvin Lee Redfern, thanks for that inherited Redfern gene that drives us to pursue our life's work, and thanks for always being there with me throughout the years encouraging me and never faltering in your belief that I could accomplish my goal.

To his loving wife Diane, for opening your linen and china cupboards and allowing us to use all of your loveliest things, and thanks too for always listening. And to your good friend, Carole Bergeron, sincere appreciation for the use of your family heirlooms and treasures as props, along with the collectibles of Lisa Redfern, Bonnie Ramsey, Juanita Queiban, and my Grandma Johnson.

To my mother, Shirley Redfern, for sharing with me your love of cook books and assistance with proof-reading, along with the help of your good friend Marylou Barkley.

With sincere appreciation I thank my good friend Joan Chevalier, for all the text editing and managing to come to visit while on vacation at just the right time…

Special thanks to Greg Hamper, for being such an incredible father to Kris and Jessica and putting me through baking school.

To my loving son, Kris Hamper, thanks for being the best son a mother could ever have, for the pride I feel every day when I think of you, for the sacrifices you have made throughout the years, and for marrying your beautiful wife, Holly. I love you both very much.

Jessica Hamper, for staying as sweet as you have always been and turning into the incredible young woman you are. For always believing in me and being excited. I love you very much!

To my brother Tom Redfern, for typing my recipes before I knew how to use a computer and helping me build my bakeries, and to Jane Redfern, Nancy Ferran and Jerry Redfern, for the help and support.

Thanks to my Aunt Adell and Uncle Bob, for taking me in and sharing your life…and your favorite recipes.

I would also like to thank the following for their recipe contributions: Susan Summers, Carole Gordon, Mrs. James Beard, Joan Williams, Anne Jordans and Oma.

To Sharon Brown, for all the prayers you have said with me, and to Jan Potter, Rob Minnetta, Holly Strecker, and Ron Choate, for being such good friends…thanks.

To my close and dear friend Dave LeClercq, thanks for introducing me to your wonderful family.

To Art and Jane Schulz and family, for adopting me.

My deepest love and appreciation to all, KAROL REDFERN HAMPER

ACKNOWLEDGEMENTS

Shelley's Special Thanks—To my beautiful children, Bryan, Emily and Taylor Odegard. Your love and success at being truly good people keeps me inspired and gives me endless hope. I am so proud of you! God bless you all! I love you!! Mom

Thanks to my parents, H. Wm. and Gloria J. Loud, for their loving child care and all the car pools you ran while I was working. We especially appreciate your open cupboards, Mom, and the endless array of family heirlooms and props you provided. Your never-ending enthusiasm, support and love are a blessing to us all. I love you dearly.

To my grandfather Clark Jennings, "Poppy", furniture designer extraordinaire: Thank you for teaching me so much about history and design, for your beautiful handmade gifts of love, and for hugging me tighter than anyone on earth. I miss you. To Marian Jennings, "Gran", who taught me to explore, to love life, to find fascination in history, antiques, books and people and who gave me, along with my mother, the gift of writing. You are such a treasure. I love you. You will always be my inspiration. Love, Shesh

Thank you to my loving grandparents, Harry and Clairene Loud, who left this world too soon. You gave me such unbelievable exposure to art and beauty, the textures, color and design that became my passion. "To understand shape, squint your eyes and see the shadows." You are always in my thoughts.

Thank you to Hazel Loud, my auntie, who let me play amongst the ribbons and decorations in her attic, who gave me silken pillows and porcelain vases when the other kids got toys. You taught me all about design and never lived to see me use your talent.

To my dear friend and mentor Marybell Towler, whom I owe worlds of thanks for all that you have taught me. I am eternally grateful. With love, Shell

FINE ART

Half-title J.F.Millet, THE SOWER, 1850 Museum of Fine Arts, Boston, Gift of Quincy Adams Shaw

Frontispiece Modeled in wax by Alfred Lenz, THE GLEANER Northwestern Miller, n.d.

Page 4/5 J.F.Millet, BUCKWHEAT HARVEST, 1868 Mrs. Martin Brimmer

Page 9 N.C. Wyeth, THE MILLER'S WOOING, n.d.

Page 13 J.F.Millet , SUMMER, THE GLEANERS, 1852-1853 Seattle Public Library, Private Collection

Page 47 J.M. Brock, THE JOLLY MILLER Northwestern Miller, n.d.

Page 49 George Romney, PORTRAIT OF MISS CONSTABLE, 1734-1802

Page 65 Winslow Homer, THE VETERAN IN A NEW FIELD, 1865 Metropolitan Museum of Arts

Page 302 J.F.Millet, THE ANGELUS, 1854-1859 Musee du Louvre, Paris

Page 308/308 J.F.Millet, THE GLEANERS, 1857 Musee du Louvre, Paris

Page 310 J.F.Millet, NOONDAY REST 1866 Museum of Fine Arts, Boston, Gift of Quincy Adams Shaw

ACKNOWLEDGEMENTS

BLACK AND WHITE PHOTOGRAPHS

Page 2 OMA, Ruth Leash Hamper, Courtesy The Hamper family

Page 14 Manual training domestic science. SPECIAL COLLECTIONS DIVISION,
UNIVERSITY OF WASHINGTON LIBRARIES, Nowell, UW Neg. # 2954

Page 21 Hopi Indian women grinding. SPECIAL COLLECTIONS DIVISION,
UNIVERSITY OF WASHINGTON LIBRARIES, E.S. Curtis, UW Neg. # 15290

Page 31 Windmill. UNIVERSITY OF NORTH DAKOTA, Chester Fritz Library

Page 71 Fisher Flouring Mills Co. truck. COURTESY OF THE FISHER MILLS INC.

Page 72 Lady pouring tea. SPECIAL COLLECTIONS DIVISION,
UNIVERSITY OF WASHINGTON LIBRARIES, UW Neg. # 10677

Page 101 Sunlit kitchen. STATE HISTORICAL SOCIETY OF NORTH DAKOTA, Neg. # D130

Page 102 Children's tea party. UCR/CALIFORNIA MUSEUM OF PHOTOGRAPHY,
Keystone-Mast Collection, University of California, Riverside, Neg. # WX5210

Page 122 1926 Baking demonstration. TACOMA PUBLIC LIBRARY, Richard's Studio, Neg. # A1366

Page 146 Lady in kitchen. SPECIAL COLLECTIONS DIVISION,
UNIVERSITY OF WASHINGTON LIBRARIES, UW Neg. # 11456

Page 167 Child in kitchen. UCR/CALIFORNIA MUSEUM OF PHOTOGRAPHY,
Keystone-Mast Collection, University of California, Riverside, Neg. # KU 90295

Page 168 University of Washington 1918 cooking class.
PEMCO WEBSTER & STEVENS COLLECTION, MUSEUM OF HISTORY & INDUSTRY

Page 193 Lacy Milling-From Then to Now.
COURTESY OF THE HANFORD SENTINEL AND KINGS COUNTY LIBRARY

Page 194 Men in kitchen. STATE HISTORICAL SOCIETY OF NORTH DAKOTA, Fiske, 1800

Page 221 Shawnee Milling Company. THE KANSAS STATE HISTORICAL SOCIETY, Topeka, Kansas

Page 222 Van de Kamps Bakery. REGIONAL HISTORY CENTER
UNIVERSITY OF SOUTHERN CALIFORNIA, Dick Whittington

Page 251 Women in kitchen. STATE HISTORICAL SOCIETY OF ND, Neg. # D130

Page 252 Women's pastry class. SPECIAL COLLECTIONS DIVISION,
UNIVERSITY OF WASHINGTON LIBRARIES, Nowell, Neg. # X2976

Page 272 Children's tea party. MUSEUM OF HISTORY & INDUSTRY, Neg. # 16699

THANKS TO *THE NORTHWESTERN MILLER* FOR BORDERS AND B&W PHOTOGRAPHS
ON THE FOLLOWING PAGES: Pages 3, 17, 19, 67, 121, 145, 161, 187, 204, 251, 265 and 310.

ACKNOWLEDGEMENTS

LOCATION SHOTS & PROPS

Joy Crothall- With special appreciation we wish to thank Joy Crothall for the use of her charming and classic kitchen, a baker's dream and the perfect backdrop for our romantic tale.

Betty Balcome- We are particularly grateful to our good friend Betty Balcome for allowing us to photograph in her enchanting home and for her unyielding enthusiasm which encouraged us many times throughout the years.

Nick and Sue LeClercq- With sincere gratitude we want to thank Nick and Sue for their gracious hospitality and for allowing us to dismantle their beautiful home (during the holidays!) and for your sincere, genuine, loving encouragement.

To Gary Odegard, ODEGARD LANDSCAPE DESIGN- Thank you for supporting our project with your incredibly artistic talents and creating the lovely setting for the photo sessions shot at the Odegard home.

Janie Bolton, AROUND THE BLOCK- A special thanks to Janie for allowing us the use of her beautiful shop as a backdrop for one of our photo-shoots (and the added bonus of allow us to accesorize with some of your incredible gift items). AROUND THE BLOCK is a shop of treasures, new and old. A true gift to Seattle from a very gifted lady. Make sure you visit!

SUR LA TABLE- Thanks to Shirley Collins and Seattle's premier kitchen shop for the incredible support and for allowing us to borrow such beautiful props for our photographs.

A special thanks to the following shops for the use of their treasures and antique collectibles; BEST OF ALL WORLDS, MADAME AND CO., GARDEN OF DISTINCTION, SWANSONS NURSERY, ALLIGATOR AND EDDY, PALAYO ANTIQUES, CHELSEA ANTIQUES, SILVER SWINE, MARKET PLACE ANTIQUES, MICHAEL BLACK ANTIQUES & THE ANTIQUE MALL IN ISSAQUAH.

The Novelty Flour Mill, Alki Beach, 1898

Sam M. Wylde Sr. is a third generation miller from England. His great-grandfather started the Novelty Mill, one of the original water powered mills in Seattle, Washington. His family owned business grew to be the largest flour distribution company on the West Coast, delivering all the flour for the Fisher Flour Mills. To one of the true pioneer fathers of flour here in the northwest, a special thanks to our good friend Sam, for all the support and encouragement you have given us throughout the years.

MORE TO BEAUTY

More there is to beauty
Than longing looks and sighs;
More to beauty, surely,
Than seeing with the eyes.

The wheatfield's checkered beauty
Breathes life upon the soul.
It's goodness has reflections
Like some strange gloriole.

Mark the trail of gold grain
From sweeping field to mart...
The wind in the wheat fields echo –
Listen with your heart.

– Helen Maring